Make Stuff Together

Make Stuff Together

24 Simple Projects to Create as a Family

BERNADETTE NOLL AND KATHIE SEVER

Wiley Publishing, Inc.

credits

Senior Editor
Roxane Cerda

Project Editor
Charlotte Kughen,
The Wordsmithery LLC

Editorial Manager
Christina Stambaugh

Vice President and Publisher
Cindy Kitchel

Vice President and Executive Publisher
Kathy Nebenhaus

Interior Design
Erin Zeltner

Cover Design
Wendy Mount

Photography
Katherine O'Brien

Technical Editor
Carla Hegeman Crim

Graphics
Karl Brandt
Brooke Graczyk
Cheryl Grubbs
Mark Pinto
Brent Savage

Bernadette Noll and Kathie Sever's original patterns are intended for noncommercial, personal use only and may not be used in the production of goods for sale in any quantity.

In memory of my sister Alma, who lovingly showed me that joy comes not just in the making, but in making stuff together, and who lived each day in the true belief that all is perfect — even when it doesn't feel quite so. And to Kenny, who believed and wondered, too.

—bn

To Mom, who showed me how; to Deb, who does it best; to Ramona and Arlo, who make it fun; and to Matt, who is always and ever.

—ks

acknowledgments

First of all, this book would not have been possible without all the kids who came through our classes and workshops and the parents who entrusted us with the task of teaching their children how to use a power tool with a sharp, pointy needle. Thanks for the laughs. And the fodder, too.

Thanks to all the businesses, neighbors, and friends who repeatedly responded to our request for materials: Texas Coffee Traders, Bouldin Creek Neighbors, Jack and Adam's Bicycles, John's Upholstery. And to the endless and amazing thrift stores of Austin that provided us not only with materials but also with soul-satisfying field trips.

Thanks to Austin's astounding craft community, who continuously gave us ideas, materials, props, and confirmation that the thrills of handmade are worth the time and effort. A special thanks to Rachel Hobson, who expanded our local craft community into the borderless virtual world and who connected us with Craftzine, which provided us with a virtual audience and a chance to do virtual summer camps when regular ones proved beyond our capacity.

Total appreciation and admiration go out to Katie O'Brien, who blessed us with her mastery of her photographer's tools. Thank you for making our book look so gorgeous. To Shannon, our lovely and talented stylist, who made sure our kids' outfits and fingernails were clean while simultaneously scouting out the best locations and layouts for our photo shoots. A big shout out to Dylan and Annie and Ella Jo, who generously let us take over their incredible East Austin compound and home for several days of photos. To Andrea, who crafted our lovely Future Craft silkscreen. And to the (unpaid) models who *weren't* there because they were our children: Lily, Henry, Matilda, Thea, Ella Jo, Cassie Rae, and Vanessa. You are beautiful and patient, and we are grateful to you all.

To the spirited and determined Kate McKean of Morhaim Literary Agency, who sought us out for the creation of this book. Thanks for your straightforward dedication and for your vision and skill at moving this from idea to book.

To our miraculous editor, Roxane Cerda, who understood not only the thrills and challenges of crafting, and of crafting a book, but also the thrills and challenges of motherhood and life in general. Your hand-holding and guidance throughout the process was priceless and totally cherished. And to Charlotte Kughen, who gave a personal flair to the fine art of technical editing. You blew our minds with your skills and memory! Thank you Wiley workers for your amazing, wily ways.

Big, fat, wide-open heart gratitude to the girls of Goodness; you know who you are. Without your commitment to the soul's journey and the encouragement to keep on keeping on and the belief that we could really do it even when we thought we were faking it, this book would not have come to fruition. Life is better with you.

Finally, to our families: Matt, Ramona, and Arlo Sever, and Kenny, Lucy, Otto, Esme, and Dean Noll Anderson. Thank you. Thank you for not calling us ridiculous. (Oh, wait; you might have done that once or twice.) Thank you for your patience and your belief that this was a good idea. Thank you for your ideas and your willingness to be our guinea pigs in the studio. Thank you for putting up with piles of random materials. And thank you, from the very big bottom of our hearts, for your love, which has been and always will be so crucial in anything we create.

Wiley Publishing would like to thank the following people for their invaluable help in testing projects in this book prior to publication:

 Long ladies (Kristie, Apphia, Achaia, Abigail, and Abiah) of marie-madeline studio

 Violet Craft of violetcraft.com

 Bernadette Emerson, Co-Editor and Publisher of *Rhythm of the Home* magazine

table of contents

foreword

As long as I can remember, I have been making *stuff*. Growing up in the '70s, most of the stuff consisted of macramé bracelets, papier-mâché piñatas, and sand candles at the beach on summer vacation. I was greatly influenced by family members making stuff around me. My mother sewed, my grandmother knit, my father caned chairs, my brothers drew and built and created stuff constantly. My fondest memories are those sitting around the kitchen table with my family crafting.

Today, all grown up with two boys of my own, I'm fortunate to carry on this family tradition. We live in such a busy time with so many distractions (much of them electronic), often rushing from one activity to the next. It's more important to me than ever to spend time unplugged and in the moment with my kids.

Make Stuff Together offers fun and creative projects that foster building family bonds while making cool stuff! The authors, Bernadette and Kathie, share their invaluable experience and insights about sewing and crafting with children, what's realistic and what doesn't work. Their projects utilize reclaimed materials and are often themed around values like showing appreciation, exploring nature, and celebrating milestones.

As I strive to create connections through creativity with my children, *Make Stuff Together* is just the book I need at my fingertips. Time spent together and the process of making is the best "stuff" I could ever hope to give to my children.

Betz White—
author of *Warm Fuzzies*
and *Sewing Green*

chapter 1

acquiring materials, building connection.

Throughout the years we have worked with all kinds of reclaimed materials: burlap sacks, birdseed bags, inner tubes, billboards, and more. We enjoy the challenge of coming up with uses for materials we find all around us and the challenge of finding just the right material to suit a specific project. Some of the materials we've found have surprised us with their versatility and ease-of-use, and some others have confounded us and brought us to new heights of frustration.

Though we hesitate to admit it, occasionally we have embarked on a class project without testing the materials ahead of time. What we hesitate to admit even more is that we've made this mistake more than once—even after learning the lesson the hard way. And then, sometimes, we made the mistake still again. However, working with kids and untested materials can sometimes hold great rewards as we make discoveries about the materials, the kids, or ourselves as we go along. Other times, though, the discoveries have led to some rather harrowing and hair-pulling experiences that required that we move happy hour a tad bit earlier in the day—such as right at the end of a class or a craft session, for example. But, as you'll read in the chapter on creating with kids, even those moments have brought some rewards.

Perhaps the biggest surprise of all in the acquisition of materials, though, has not been in the materials themselves or in the lessons learned in class, but in the people we encountered while acquiring the materials. What we were able to build, beyond the wallets or bags or games, was a greater sense of our surrounding community.

Some items came from people and businesses with which we had already established a relationship. The coffee roaster from whom we bought our coffee each week was more than happy to give us stacks and stacks of burlap sacks for our projects. One day we were just regular customers buying product, having the usual regular customer banter, and the next day we were fellow artisans looking behind the scenes and having lengthy discussions about our work and ourselves. The coffee roaster's interest in what we were doing both with the kids and with the materials grew, because he now had a vested interest. Hence, our connection to another person in our community—and to all the roaster's employees—was deepened.

Other connections were created because we came up with an idea for a project and were in pursuit of a specific material. The upholsterer down the street, for example, whose shop we had driven by countless times but had never stopped in, suddenly became a recognizable neighbor with whom we built an ongoing relationship. He gave us big end rolls of upholstery and promised us an infinite supply. He was happy to have a place to send his scraps rather than tossing them in the landfill, and we were happy to find a resource, so the arrangement was mutually beneficial. We also got a glimpse into a world we'd never seen before where recycling was old school and was the basis for the entire business. The upholsterer was "green" before the term had the meaning it has today. To this day, we wave as we ride by the shop, and we enjoy the new connections we have made. For us as parents, too, it's great to know that our children are seeing the people all around us as co-operators in this thing called living.

These stories have repeated themselves with other people all over town. There's the bike shop where we pick up inner tubes and event banners. The sign company where we've gotten outdated billboards. The neighborhood list where we put out a call for bird seed bags. There are all sorts of people and businesses who are part of our community who we would not have met if we hadn't been trying to find sources for materials. Even when we've acquired something for a one-shot deal, which is often the case, the connections we've made are everlasting and the conversations ongoing. And the lessons of Bernadette's mom have been proven true time and time again: "If it's worth having, it's worth asking for." How great that our kids can learn the lesson about speaking up and asking for what they need while they're still so young.

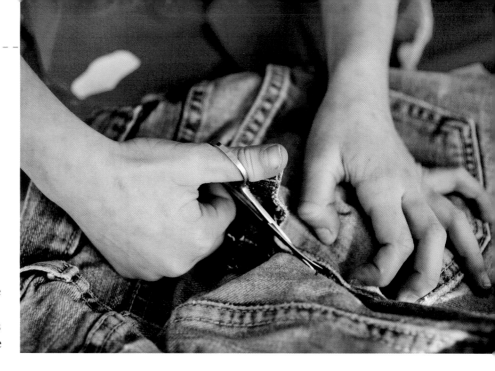

What we've learned is that there is more than just green living in upcycling or reusing materials. There is a lesson in the human experience and the understanding that, although we might all be in pursuit of different things and live completely different lives, ultimately we are all connected. We're not saying we've found the meaning of life through this process; actually, maybe we are saying that.

Do you remember that song the folks on *Sesame Street* used to sing about community? "Who are the people in your neighborhood, they're in your neighborhood, they're in your neighborhoo-ood. Who are the people in your neighborhood? The people that you meet each day." That's kind of how it feels for us and for the kids, too. That our neighborhood grows with each new person that we meet.

We've provided a list of materials and places you might find them, but it is by no means comprehensive. What we find all the time is that there are always new possibilities out there that can be salvaged into a craft and there are new connections to be made with the people all around you. So, look at our list and then look around your house and your town and your alley ways to see what's out there just beckoning to be run through the sewing machine. And who's out there just beckoning to be met.

- **Burlap bags**—Any coffee roaster has burlap bags and will be more than happy to have you take the bags off his or her hands. While you're there you can pick up some coffee grinds for your compost pile, too.
- **Bird seed bags/pet food bags**—If you don't buy bird seed or pet food of your own, put a call out to your neighbors or local pet store. We have found many folks who are happy to stockpile bags for us so that we can use them on a whole mess of projects. (Not messy projects, but a mess of projects.) There is one particular bird-loving elderly woman in our neighborhood who is happy to know the bags are being used, happy to know children are learning to sew, and happy, too, for the random visits she gets when we pick up materials.
- **Billboards**—Call your local sign company to ask about availability. Sometimes there is a small fee, but the fee is usually negligible compared to the size of the material. Think billboards. *Gigantic.* And sometimes pretty cool prints, too—especially when dissected into smaller parts.
- **Inner tubes**—Any bike shop will be *happy* to save these for you. Inner tubes are hard to run through the sewing machine, but they make great bag handles because they're stretchy and durable.
- **Event banners**—Bike shops, running shops, and convention centers are great places to check for old banners that need a new home. Nowadays more businesses are trying to make signs that can be re-used year after year, but mostly the signs are used only one time and then need to be discarded.

- **Fabric sample books**—Upholstery shops have these by the boatloads. If you're lucky to have a boat upholstery shop in your community, the vinyl samples are pretty darn cool for a whole lot of projects. And they, too, are happy to know that there are young kids learning how to sew.
- **Upholstery end rolls**—Most upholsterers have piles of pieces of upholstery (home décor) fabric that are too small for their needs but are still plenty big for many projects. We recommend that you call first to ask the upholsterer to save the scraps, but oftentimes you can just pop in to pick up whatever is on hand. Worst case scenario is that you pop in and the upholsterer has nothing. You still get the chance for a visit.
- **Neoprene**—Mostly we find old wet suits at thrift stores—there are a surprising number of them available. Dive shops sometimes have old wet suits that they are willing to offer for free or cheap. Oftentimes, too, they have sales of used equipment where you can find giant neoprene suits; the bigger the better! When else would you and your child get a chance to visit a dive store?
- **Linens/towels/wool blankets**—Thrift stores are *loaded* with old linens, towels, and blankets. In fact, one of our favorite local thrift stores has "half-price linen day" every Monday. Garage sales also almost always have piles of linens that are just waiting to be scooped up for just a little money! You can also ask around your neighborhood as most folks have an odd sheet here and there that they'd be more than happy to donate to an upcycling project. Think how fun it would be to have a designated day of walking through the neighborhood with your kiddos and your little wagon to pick up the linens people have saved for you.

You'll see as you peruse the projects that many of our projects require only small pieces of cloth. Part of this came about because we had buckets of small scraps left over from various other endeavors; scraps too big to toss but too small to use for many sewing projects. Most of these scraps were from favorite fabrics, which is partly why we saved them rather than tossing them. Look in your own scrap bins or put a call out to sewers or crafters you know. Many of them will be *thrilled* to find someone who actually wants you to use their beloved scraps from their not always beloved scrap buckets. If you want to get really ingenious, sew smaller pieces together in random order to create larger fabric swatches.

Get creative with your resources and creative with your material choices, too. Encourage your kids to join in the task of collecting and ask them to look around at what materials they see as they make their way through the world. Children can learn so much from looking outside their own world, thinking outside the box in pursuit of materials. In turn we can learn so much from them.

And if you find something really cool to use in your projects, or some undiscovered resource for materials, let us know. We're always on the prowl for new upcycling ideas.

Theodore Roosevelt summed it up in a way when he said, "Do what you can. Where you are. With what you have." That's kind of what we're talking about.

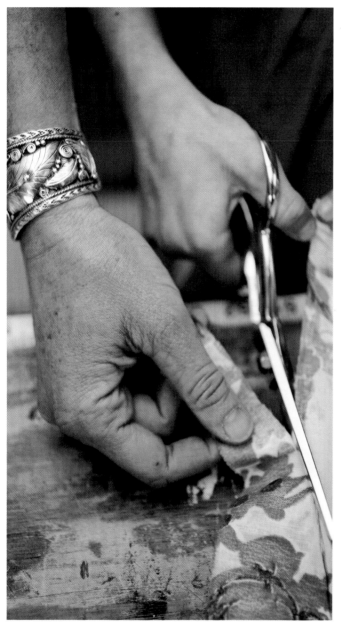

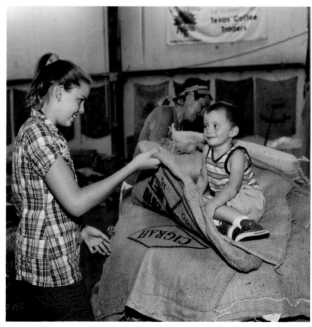

the ways and whys of making stuff together

W e have always loved the idea of making stuff with our kids. We have had visions of the whole family working side-by-side on group projects with objects of great beauty being the end result. In reality there was, and is, a rather large learning curve to calmly making stuff with kids. Although we'd like to say that we now have only peaceful, easy crafting sessions with our kids and projects that turn out exactly as in our visions, it'd be a Big Fat Lie.

However, we have learned some things over the years that have resulted in more occasions where everyone is getting their craft on, happily and serenely, and everyone is enjoying the process of making stuff together or alone, as the case may be. We are each able, on occasion, to let go of our own vision and join in a collective vision instead. What we've learned has been one of the driving forces of this whole book because we feel the information we have gleaned can really take a lot of pressure off parents and children who somehow believe that everyone else always has an easy, loving, hyper-creative time of it. So we're sharing what we've discovered with you so that you might benefit from our trial—and our error, too.

We'd like to say that the tricks we learned were about ways to get our children to do exactly what we want them to do. Really, though, the biggest trick has been training ourselves to let go of crazy expectations in the craft room. It might sound harsh when we say that you should go into a crafting project with your kids with no expectations, but it's perhaps the biggest truth we hold as parents—the idea of expecting nothing. We present all our ideas and materials and patterns to our kids with gusto and then just let go. At the same time we have to accept whatever comes our way. It's easier said than done, we know. As hard as it might be, though, it is definitely easier than not letting go and trying to overly control our children's creativity.

There are a lot of reasons why you might want to craft with your kids. Crafting builds connection, fosters creativity, provides occupation for a rainy afternoon, or maybe just gives you something to send to Grandma. Whatever your reasons for crafting, you need to make sure that love of the process comes before love of the final product. If you only keep your eyes on the prize of the finished project and have expectations about how it will look in the end, you might need to find some time to have a little solo craft period instead. You should know there is absolutely nothing wrong with solo crafting. In fact, it's quite the opposite. The important thing is to realize what you need ahead of time rather than realizing it midway through a cranky craft session with your kids.

So, the first part of making stuff together is asking yourself, "Do I really want to do this project with my kids?" If the answer is yes, go for it and enjoy the process. If the answer is no, find something else that you can create together that will bring you the most amount of connection and fun and satisfaction in the time you spend together. Perhaps a different craft project or a different medium, such as chalk drawings on the sidewalk, would be a more rewarding group project. Then you can go ahead and make the project *you* want on your own. A little adult-only crafting time might be just the thing you need to carry on with the crazy job of parenting.

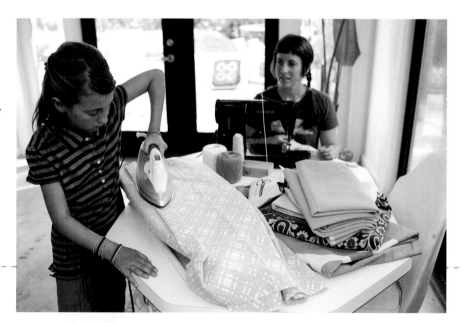

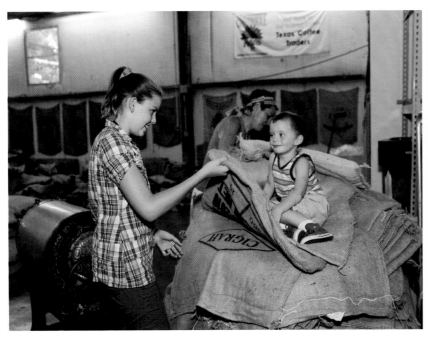

Tips for Crafting with Kids

If you have made the decision and the commitment to craft with kids, here are some things we've discovered about creating a peaceful and fun experience when you're making stuff together:

⭐ Remember that the process, not the finished product, is the goal. As we stated earlier, if you have a clear and definite vision of how something should look in the end, make it yourself.

⭐ Although sewing is different than a random art session in the sense that sewing requires that you use patterns and power tools, make sure to allow a little time for free expression. Inject your projects with as much creativity as you can. Even when there is a pattern to be followed, have fun with the process of choosing fabrics and embellishments and allow a little time for some improvisation, too.

⭐ When crafting with kids, decide ahead of time what your boundaries are. Just because your girlfriend lets her kids go crazy with craft sessions doesn't mean the same approach works for you. Find your comfort zone. Do you love a little chaos? Then by all means, go for it. Do you feel panicked by too much pandemonium? Then set clear boundaries and spell them out for your kids. Your kids can have chaos on their own time or when they visit your girlfriend and her kids.

⭐ You can apply boundaries to your material and medium choices, too. If you are freaked out by permanent markers or acrylic paint, choose something else. Watercolors versus acrylics. Colored pencils versus permanent markers. Find your comfort zone so that your focus can be on the process rather than the panic that sets in as you watch your kids use the supplies. If this makes you feel like you're being too controlling, try a different location. Or try to push yourself a little to let go. If that's too hard, but you still really want to figure out a way to let go a little bit, don't watch so closely. Get yourself involved in your own process and let the kids work independently on theirs. If you still can't quite get there, but you *want* to, find another parent who might do it with you. It can be comforting to have another adult present.

⭐ Don't cram in a craft session when time is limited. Allowing enough time for the project at hand brings about way more peace, love, and happiness.

Work in an area that works for you. Maybe the kitchen table suits you just fine. Or maybe outdoors is where you need to be. Where you work it needs to feel right or it will definitely feel wrong. Choosing the right area can also help you push your own boundaries a little if that's what you desire.

Minimize materials. Don't overwhelm your kids with too many piles or too many choices. When working with kids, or anyone really, having too many choices can make a kid feel like he or she will never be able to make the right decision. With this feeling comes a sense of diminished satisfaction in the end product. Too few choices, though, can leave a kid feeling imprisoned by the lack of possibilities. Strike a comfortable balance for yourself and for your kids by allowing room to explore without overwhelming.

Employ "the cobbler and the elves" solution when necessary. If your children are stuck on a project—a mess of tangled threads or fabric gone all wonky or stitches that are stitched the wrong direction—and they are to the point of throwing up their hands and abandoning the project altogether, you can help by giving them just a little leg up. We're not saying run in and rescue their work whenever there's trouble. Instead, reserve this method for those times when all hope for completion of the project is lost if you don't help a little.

You can help quietly when they're out playing or sleeping or maybe just out of the room for a few minutes. With a little intervention you can help the kids by leaving the project in a state that entices them to pick it up again and get to work. Think of it as helping your child climb a tree. We're not saying you should lift them up and stick them in the branches. Just give them a foothold so that they can then use their own power to boost themselves the rest of the way. Sometimes a tiny boost is all that's needed to get the child back in the game.

Our final tip is this: When you work with kids, try to remember that not everything is sacred. Learning the power of editing is a lifelong skill regardless of our craft—be it writing, cooking, sewing, or carpentry. It's okay to delete an entire paragraph, compost a bad combination of ingredients, rip out a seam, or take out a wall. You have to do whatever needs to be done in order to make the project what you want. In the end, if the project is deemed just plain undesirable, teach your kids the joys of redoing it or getting rid of it altogether. There's a thrill in altering, editing, or ditching something you've made, and it teaches kids that, although joy can definitely be found in the final product, another joy is found in the process of making stuff. Together.

Technical Notes About Using the Patterns in This Book

For all of the projects in this book we use ½" seam allowance unless otherwise noted, and even that has a little wiggle room if need be.

We also encourage you to utilize small scraps of fabric that you already have on hand. Because many of the projects only require small pieces, we've provided measurements in inches so that you can determine if you have a scrap that's large enough for the project. (We've also given measurements in yardage in case you have to buy new material.) Whenever possible, use leftovers from other projects, old shirts, tablecloths, bed sheets, or whatever you have around the house that will work. Play around. Mix it up. Utilize your scraps. You know you have some!

Project Layout

The projects in this book are broken into three parts. We came up with this method because we realized that oftentimes, as parents, we try to cram just a little bit more into a timeslot than is really feasible or pleasant. Originally we created three-day projects, but that method felt too dogmatic. Three parts leaves it more in your hands. When we break things down into smaller segments and allow a bit more spaciousness of time and place, things flow a little bit better.

In Bernadette's work with Slow Family Living, the motto is *slow down, connect, enjoy.* It's about the idea of taking a pause long enough to catch a breath and to figure out what's happening and what's needed. It's about really seeing each other and finding the connection in the big and small parts, which then enables us to truly enjoy the many aspects of family life.

This same idea is true for crafting as well: Slow down—long enough to ponder materials, space, moods, blood sugar levels, and so on. Connect—check in with yourself. Look at each other and state some intentions about how you want to feel in this process. From there, enjoy—enjoy the time, the process, the projects, and the people with whom you're working.

Of course, if you have time and space many of these projects can be finished in one session. In some of them the steps aren't about an actual part of a craft but a part of family life. We know that family life can sometimes be difficult or feel too busy or disconnected. We also know that when we slow down long enough to check in with ourselves and be more intentional and thoughtful, we are more able to find the joy in things.

We hope you have fun with these projects and with what they bring to your family life. We'd love for you to send us pictures. Let us know what lessons you've learned. Because one thing's for sure: In family life the lessons just keep coming and coming!

chapter 3

dinner time

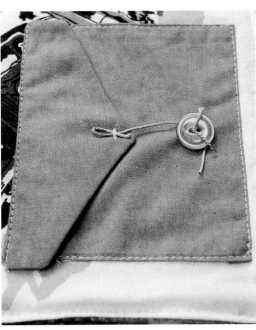

Before we had children, the idea of family dinner time conjured up images of long hours sitting around the kitchen table with everyone peacefully sharing tales of the day and enjoying the repast set before them. Actuality, however, has been something else completely as real life called, tired toddlers objected before we even began, and older kids were called away to homework, books, play, rest, or other obligations of the day. Even in the face of the struggles, however, we have been unwilling to completely let go of family dinner as a ritual in both of our homes.

After many struggles to hold onto our (unrealistic) visions of fancy family dinners, with tidy, well-behaved children eating exotic and well-prepared feasts, we have finally realized that what we seek from this time together, aside from sustenance, of course, is connection—a moment in the day to be together as a family. And by moment, we mean just that: a moment. Whether we have an hour or fifteen minutes, no matter how busy life might be or how tired we might feel, we have learned that we can get the small snippets of connection we want without perfect meals or flawlessly behaving children. Instead, we can inject small and simple rituals and use clever tools to make whatever time we have around the table feel worthwhile. And even the times it doesn't feel all that peaceful, at least we feel like we're setting the stage for future dinners together with our grown children who have these rituals as an intrinsic part of their very being.

The sharing of high points and low points, which can take a few minutes or all evening depending on what we need and want, can make our time together feel complete and give us a glimpse into each other's days. A round of appreciations or a moment of silence, and the meal, wherever it goes from there, fills us up on some level. Believe us when we tell you it doesn't always present exactly as we envision, but sometimes it does. And we accept the *sometimes* as good enough.

As we laid out the projects in this chapter, we looked at our own experiences with our real-life families and our real-life dinners. What are the things that actually make us want to be there eating and sharing night after night? What do we do that makes us return to the table? What brings us a feeling of connection? We realized it was the sharing of not only the meal but the shared prep of the table, too. And when the objects and rituals are familiar and routine such as candles, napkins, water, and so on, it makes it easier for everyone, even the wee ones, to participate to some degree. Moods permitting, of course. The projects in this chapter are about creating things to bring to the table; these are the things that work for us. This chapter is a chance also to ponder what it's all about for *you and your* family. What do you like? What do you need? What works for you?

After many years and many meals during which we've begged our kids to do something our way or love the foods we love, we have finally figured out that all we can really control is ourselves. Though we have tried—oh my, how we have tried—we can't control the mood of the kids or their reception of the foods. So, what do we parents bring to the table? We bring not just the tangible things, such as dishes and meals, but we bring other even more important things, such as emotions, conversations, rituals, and ideas. These are the parts we want our children to remember. The things that bring us together. Even though they might protest some of them on occasion, we can really see that overall, they like the routines and the feeling of familiarity—in the truest sense of the word. We hope, of course, that in years to come, as our children prepare meals with their own partners (if they have them) and their own children (if they have them) that some of these routines will be remembered. Maybe not the actual thing or habit, but the feeling of connection we all get.

So as you make your own family dinners, serve smoothies and cereal if that's what you need to do. Or serve a crown roast lovingly prepared with all the fixings if you like. Although the food should be healthy, the food is not what makes a meal the *family dinner*. What gives the family dinner the value is the connection, the ritual, and the tradition. And, as we go through all this effort to feed and connect on a daily basis, we can try to have fun. Because if we have fun and try to enjoy it on some level, that's what our families see. And really, who can resist a little fun and joy?

Personalized Napkin Rings
and Cloth Napkins

Personalized Napkin Rings and Cloth Napkins

In both of our households, we use cloth napkins so that we're not using up piles of paper napkins at every meal. The cloth napkins cover a whole lot more territory than the paper variety ever could on faces, hands, and table top (when there's a spill emergency). And, on a set table, cloth napkins add a pleasing aesthetic that is oh-so-important when dining as a family. There's a lot of mess in family life. Anytime we can add aesthetic pleasure, we all benefit.

In order to keep the laundry minimized, we use personalized napkin rings for our napkins so that we can establish ownership, an essential aspect of dining with children, and get some reuse out of the slightly dirty napkins.

The personalization has been useful also in establishing seating preferences, an unintended bonus when setting the family table. In one of our households (the one with four kids) the rule about seating is setter's choice. And don't you think the setter just loves reigning over the table with the napkins clutched tightly in fist?

• **Finished Measurements: Rings:** 2" diameter; **Napkins:** 9 12" × 12" •

Supplies

One long piece of heavy cardboard tubing

1 yard of 45" wide, light- to medium-weight cotton fabric yields either 9 12" × 12" or 12 12" × 11" napkins.

Low temp glue gun and glue sticks

Buttons (optional)

Scrap fabric of any variety, pieces need to be at least 5" × 9" or so to fit most napkin ring tubes. If purchasing fabric, ¼ yard is enough for at least 8 napkin rings.

Rubber stamps and stamp pad (optional)

Hacksaw or utility knife or any other type of saw

Note: *For our tubing, we used the tube from a fabric roll. You could also use heavy tape rolls or the tube from a large roll of paper. You can ask at an upholstery shop or a large scale print shop for their discards. Mailing tubes are also a good option, and can be purchased at office supply shops. For the light- to medium-weight fabric, we actually used an old tablecloth.*

Part One

This cloth napkin project is small and easy so neither the time nor the space required is huge. Depending on how many kids you have and the ages of each one, this entire project should take just about an hour or two, maybe more if your family is prone to a lot of talking and jockeying for position.

You need enough room for laying out your cloth. A table around which everyone can stand is great, so if you are doing this project at the kitchen table you might want to pull the chairs away and put out a small step stool for the wee ones.

Steps

1. Iron your fabric. This is often a good job for kids who are the right height for the ironing board. When closely supervised, even kids as young as three can wield an iron, and they love going back and forth making the fabric go from wrinkly to smooth.

2. Lay the fabric out on the table. If you are working with more than one child, have the kids stand on each side of the table to spread it out evenly.

3. Measure and mark as many 12" × 12" squares as you need. This is a great job for the kids because it doesn't really matter whether it's straight or the perfect length or anything. In fact, this is a good time to step away and let the kids have at the process on their own. For really little kids, a cardboard pattern piece might make marking the squares easier.

4. On a scrap piece of fabric practice with the kids the art of tearing fabric. By just cutting one little snip perpendicular to the edge, the fabric can then be torn very effectively (and very satisfyingly) in a straight line. Tearing fabric feels really good and makes a great sound as well. (Insert theatrical pants ripping pantomime here.) Now have the kids do this for real on the napkin pieces they marked.

5. Hem the edges of each square. You can either have the kids iron down a double-folded ¼" hem and then sew or, if you have the proper foot and the know-how, simply sew a rolled hem at the machine. You can also use a serger to create a rolled hem.

6. Now it's time to tidy things up and get outside and play. Or make dinner. Or fold yet another load of your Sisyphus-like piles of laundry.

Part Two

The napkin ring project is pretty fun (and it's also just pretty). It involves a little slicing, a little hot gluing, and a little sewing as well. What more could a kid ask for? You can personalize the napkin rings using rubber stamps or by choosing different buttons or just by having them be done in different fabric prints. Let the kids decide how they want to individualize their napkin rings. Don't forget to make a couple extra for guests.

Steps

1. Cut the cardboard tubing into slices approximately 2" wide. Let the (supervised) kids cut the pieces using a hacksaw or utility knife. If you have a chop saw, that works really great, too, although that turns this into a task for an adult.

2. Measure the width of each slice. Double that measurement and add ¾" to accommodate the seam allowance and thickness of the tube. If the slices are all different widths, complete this step for each individual piece. This is a good math equation for a kid.

3. Measure the circumference of the tube and add 1¼" for the seam allowance and for the fold. Steps 2 and 3 are the measurements for your fabric scraps.

4. Check your math. For example, if your tube slice is 2" × 7" then your fabric would be 4¾" × 8¼". Cut a piece of scrap fabric that is appropriately sized for each piece of tube.

5. Slice each piece of tube so that it can be opened, not unlike one of those cheap kid's adjustable rings you get from the gum ball machine.

6. Fold the fabric lengthwise with the right sides together. Stitch along one short end and down the long side, ¼" from the edges. Snip the seam allowances at the corners.

7. Turn your fabric right side out.

8. Slide your fabric onto your ring of cardboard. If it is too tight to easily slide on your fabric, you can trim your cardboard tube. Make sure you get the tube all the way to the stitched end of the fabric. You should have a tail when the fabric is all the way on the piece of tube (see the illustration).

Extra flap with raw edge

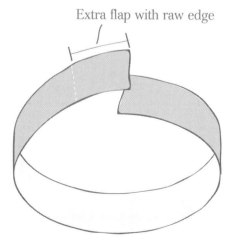

9. Double fold the tail end to make a flap, fold the flap toward the middle of the tube circle (away from the cut edge), and glue it into place. This hides the raw edges of the fabric.

Double fold the tail to make a flap

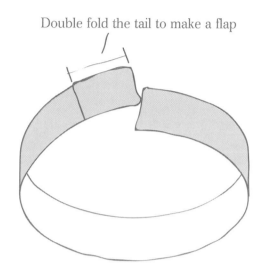

Fold flap back and glue in place

10. If you'd like, glue a button onto the fold. This not only looks pretty but also draws attention away from the bulkiness of your fold.

Glue on decorative button

11. Let everyone stamp his or her own ring using letter stamps or other designs.

12. Get everyone on board for a tidy-up by offering a little treat upon completion. There is absolutely nothing wrong with a well placed bribe, or, as they call it in the corporate world, an incentive.

Declaring a little ownership of the design elements helps everyone remember whose napkin is whose,

which ensures that you don't accidentally end up sharing a napkin with your very sweet, though messy, 10-year-old boy.

Part Three

Now you've got your rings and napkins, you can have a little family discussion about why you use cloth napkins. What are the benefits? Talk about paper napkins versus cloth. How many napkins would your family use in the course of a year if every person uses two paper napkins every day?

What is the history of the napkin ring? Did you know there is documentation of the napkin ring dating all the way to the 1500s? Though we use them now to minimize wash, we also use them to minimize germs. Why was the prevention of germ spreading so much more crucial in ancient times?

While you're at it, why not create your family's chore chart so that there's no discussion about whose turn it is to set the table each night. In Bernadette's house, they have the jobs on a weekly rotation rather than switching every day. That way there's less wondering from day to day about who is to do what.

Blessing and Sharing Pouch

Blessing and Sharing Pouch

The dinner hour can sometimes be the only time during the day when we all gather in one spot with a clear view of each family member. Of course, the dinner hour can also sometimes feel a little rushed or kooky, especially if we are coming in from elsewhere or hurrying in order to get to something. It is for this reason that we are fans of having an intentional kickoff for the meal to avoid letting chaos or crankiness rule.

The idea of a blessing, a moment of silence, or the chiming of the gong indicates to every family member that whatever we were doing before is finished for now because we are now on to dinner, together, as a family. Most of the time it works. And the moment of silence might just be the only moment of silence in the house all day long.

In addition to the blessing, we are fans of using sharing prompts to stimulate conversation. This isn't because anyone really needs encouragement to talk, but because sharing prompts provide an equitable way for each person to get his or her turn to share. It's also a nice way for everyone to learn the fine art of listening, which is an ongoing practice for sure.

Note: *We have a variety of themes we use for sharing something about our days out there in the world as separate beings. Sometimes we do high points and low points, which offers each of us a chance to really reflect on what we did out in the world that day. It feels right to acknowledge not just the highs, but the lows, too, so that we all have a true sense of each other's experiences. It can serve as a way of processing or resolving something that was hard or sad or made us mad. Sometimes after the bad things have been spoken out loud, they are diffused somewhat and we can move on.*

Other themes we use include appreciations nights, sharing funny stories, or describing beauty we saw in the world on that day. The topics don't really matter. The main idea is that through talking, listening, and giving the dinner gathering a bit of intention, we are building an understanding of each other and the connection we all seek.

● **Finished Measurements:** 15" × 7" pouch ●

Supplies

¼ yard (or scrap larger than 16" × 8") of burlap for outer pouch

¼ yard (or scrap larger than 16" × 8") of medium-weight fabric for the inner pouch

¼ yard of quilt-weight cotton for the pockets and tie

2 medium buttons (¾" to 1" in diameter)

1 foot of hemp twine

Embroidery floss (for tying on the buttons)

Needle that has a big enough eye to accommodate the floss, but is narrow enough to fit through the holes in the button

Note: *For the medium-weight fabric, we used a piece of tablecloth that we had left from making the napkins and the napkin basket from the other projects in this chapter. You could also use home décor fabric, canvas, or even soft denim.*

Part One

Depending on the ages of children you're dealing with, this segment can take about an hour or so. This is a good activity for Friday night or Saturday morning. If you have little ones in your house, have them try their hands at cutting the burlap and the twine. Or, you can give them a scrap of fabric to practice cutting while you cut the pieces for the pouch. If you need something to keep your kids engaged but they're not quite able to really participate, teach them the joy of pulling strands of the jute out of the burlap cloth one by one. That is so darn satisfying for some reason, and it requires some good concentration for a little kid (or a zoned-out adult).

Steps

1. Cut a 16" × 8" rectangle from the burlap for the outside of the pouch.

2. Cut a 16" × 8" rectangle from the medium-weight fabric for the inside of the pouch.

3. Cut two 5" × 6" rectangles from the quilt-weight cotton. These are your pockets.

4. Cut four pieces of the quilt-weight cotton using the pattern piece from page 141. These are your pocket flaps.

5. Cut a 42" × 2" strip of the quilt-weight cotton for the tie.

6. Cut two 6" pieces of twine.

Part Two

Now it's time for some sewing! The sewing tasks on this day are good for kids because the smallness of the pieces makes them less intimidating. Also, if the sewing gets majorly messed up, you can always just recut your fabric and start over.

The steps in this part apply to both pockets on the inside of the pouch.

Steps

1. For each flap: Put a pair of the flap pieces together with the right sides facing. Using a ¼" seam allowance, stitch almost all the way around the perimeter of the piece leaving a small opening in the center of the top long edge for turning. Trim the seam allowance at the corners and point to reduce bulk. Repeat for the other flap.

2. Turn the pocket flaps right side out. Tuck the edges into place at the top and press.

3. Pinch a small loop in the end of the twine. Machine stitch the twine in place on the front of the pocket flap about ¼" from the bottom point as shown in the illustration. Be sure to sew back and forth over the loop several times to be sure your twine is secure.

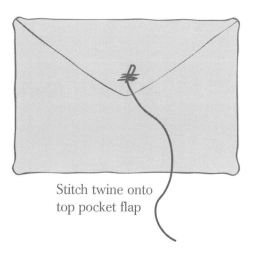

Stitch twine onto top pocket flap

4. For both pocket pieces, fold the short edges over ¼" to the wrong side and press. Fold one of the long edges over ¼", fold the remaining long edge over ½", and press; this is the top of the pocket. Stitch the top of the pocket into place ¼" from your turned-down top edge.

5. Center your button about 1" from the bottom folded edge of the pocket. Insert the embroidery floss into the needle, and use it to "tie" the button into place (see the illustration and refer to the appendix for more information).

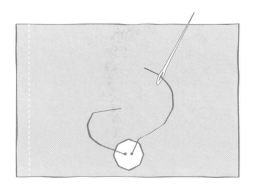

6. Place your medium-weight inner pouch piece on your work surface and designate a "top" and a "bottom." (We made our decision based on the print of the fabric.) Pin each pocket onto the medium-weight fabric ¾" from the bottom and 1" from a side edge, making sure that your pocket is oriented correctly with the top edge toward the top of the medium-weight fabric.

7. Starting at the top of one corner, stitch around the three sides of each pocket. Use a ⅛" seam allowance, and be sure to backstitch at the beginning and end.

8. Pin the long edge of the pocket flap to the medium-weight fabric about ½" above the top of the pocket.

9. Stitch down the pocket flap into place ⅛" from the top edge.

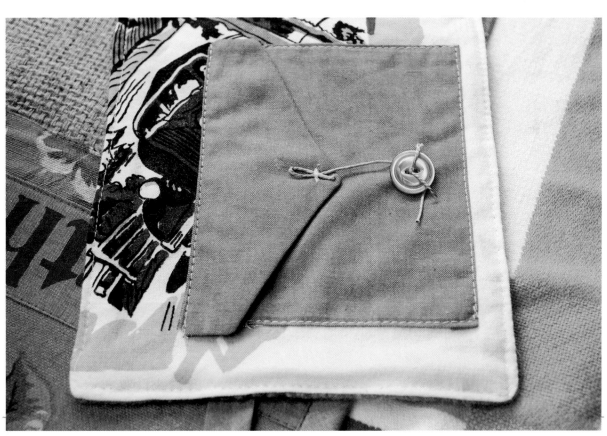

Part Three

When we sew with children there are some moments of extreme frustration, but there are also moments of magic. One of those magic times is the turning of an item that has been sewn with wrong sides together and then top-stitching the piece. The piece goes from being rather ugly and seemingly messy to perfectly clean, flat, and flawless. Get ready to experience that magic.

Steps

1. Fold the 42" × 2" piece of cotton in half lengthwise with the right sides together to create a long, skinny piece.

2. Using a ¼" seam allowance, sew along one of the short edges and then turn and sew down the long edge. As you approach the center of the long edge, lift your needle, leave a gap of about two inches and then begin sewing again. After finishing the long edge, turn and sew the second short edge. Trim the seam allowance around the corners.

3. Using a turning tool such as a chopstick or a knitting needle, push the ends of the tie out through the opening to turn it right side out.

4. Press the strip flat, making sure you tuck in the raw edges of the gap that was left open from turning the strip right side out.

5. Place your burlap piece on your work surface and then center your pouch tie horizontally about 3" from the top long edge. (You can determine which the top is by looking at your burlap piece and deciding which edge you'd like to be the top.) Pin the tie to the burlap.

6. Starting 1" from the short edge of the burlap, stitch the tie in place ⅛" from the long edge of the tie. When you're 1" from the other short edge of the burlap pivot and sew across the tie, then turn and edge stitch down the second long edge of the tie (see the illustration). When you are in line with the beginning of the stitching, pivot and stitch across to that point.

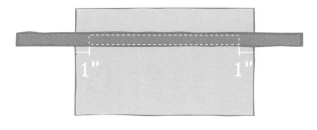

7. Make a few folds in the ties and secure with pins in the center of the burlap piece. This keeps them out of the way of the stitching. Align the medium-weight fabric and the burlap pieces with the wrong sides together and pin.

8. Starting in the middle of one long side, stitch ½" from the edges. Leave an opening of 2" or 3" for turning. Run a second row of stitching in the seam allowance just beside the first row to prevent fraying during the turning process. Trim the seam allowance to ¼" at the corners.

9. Turn your piece right side out.

10. Tuck in the edges of the opening and press. Stitch all the way around the four sides, about ⅛" from the edges. Be sure to catch the edges of the opening in your stitches. Remove the pins to release the ties.

Now that you are finished sewing, you can get to work on your prompts. At the next family dinner discuss what kind of things you want to put on your family's cards. What's important to you as a family? What do you want to know about everyone's day? Write the suggestions on small pieces of cardstock or cardboard and put them in the pockets.

Burlap Cloth-Lined Basket

Burlap Cloth-Lined Basket

This utilitarian little basket provides a storage and carrying vessel for your family's dinner napkins and napkin rings so that even the youngest member of the family can bring what's needed to the table.

On our walls at home we have thorough (though sometimes ignored) job charts that hang where everyone can see them. And we admit also that even though the charts hang quite visibly, not everyone chooses to see them until he or she is pointed directly at the chart. One of the jobs is table setting, which requires that all the detritus a family can leave on any horizontal space in the home first be cleared from the table. One item that stays on the table is this burlap basket, which holds all our clean and ready-to-use napkins and rings. It's handy to have it there and somehow it makes the task of setting the table seem not quite so daunting to whoever has that particular assignment that week.

Note: *If you make one of these and leave it on your table, make sure that it doesn't become a "catch-all." Just that word alone says enough. Catch-alls don't feel good. It might seem like a good idea when a catch-all begins to form, but after the "all" part enters into it, it is impossible to find anything in the pile. It then becomes necessary to create yet another catch-all somewhere else in the home until eventually you are surrounded by catch-alls, and you're unable to find anything you need.*

This project requires a little more attention to detail than the other dinner projects and so it might be the one that you do with older kids or maybe, just maybe, you could do this one on your own some afternoon when all the family is out at a soccer game or a birthday party. As much as we like sharing our love of crafting with the kids, there are those solo crafting moments that are oh-so-satisfying. And, of course, if you do choose to do it with the kids, you still might choose to do some parts yourself and other parts with the kids.

• **Finished Measurements:** 10" L × 10" W × 7½" H •

Supplies

Burlap bag or ½ yard of 60" wide burlap (off the bolt) for the outside of the basket and the divider.

Medium- to heavy-weight fabric for the inside of the basket (we used the same fabric we used for the napkins). If the fabric width is 53" or greater, you need ½ yard. If the fabric width is less than 53", you need ¾ yard.

Part One

The only prep required for this part of the project might be getting all the kids in bed at a decent hour so you can sit at your table, scissors in hand, cutting pieces, with a good podcast playing in the background. You could also do this solo by giving little kids some fabric to cut on their own to get them in the practice of cutting.

Cutting burlap is way easier for little kids than cutting other fabric because of its heft and its lines. If you want to keep kids busy, you can show them how to pull strands one by one from the burlap so they can make a big bird's nest of burlap strings. Whether the kids are doing the project with you or doing something similar next to you, the connection is there, and that's the goal. Right?

Steps

1. Cut one 41" × 8" strip of burlap for the outside sides.

2. Cut one 11" × 11" square of burlap for the outside bottom.

3. Cut one 10½" × 13" rectangle of burlap for the divider.

4. Cut one 41" × 11½" piece of fabric for the inside sides.

5. Cut one 11" × 11" square of fabric for the outside bottom.

Part Two

This basket is made up of separate pieces that you make and then join together. Just like family dinner itself! All the separate beings come together to sit at one table and make up one big, sometimes loud, sometimes wonky, sometimes happy, always a family, family.

Note: When you're sewing burlap it is a good idea to run two rows of stitches side by side along the edges to prevent the burlap from fraying.

Steps

1. Bring the short ends of the long burlap strip together. Stitch together, ½" from the short edges.

2. Press the seam allowance open and sew each side into place ¼" from the seam to reinforce the stitching. Turn the loop right side out so that the seam allowances are on the inside.

3. Arrange the loop so that the seam is 5" from one of the side folds. Press the side folds to make nice creases.

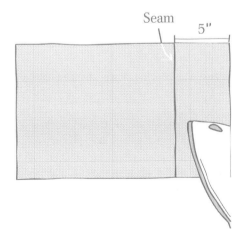

Seam   5"

4. Rearrange the loop so that the creases are in line in the center. Press the newly formed side folds.

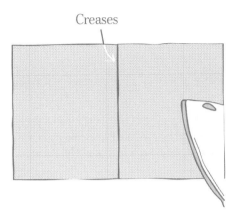

Creases

5. Decide which of the raw edges should be at the bottom of the basket. Make a ½" snip at the position of each crease at the bottom edge.

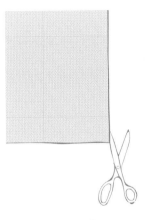

6. Turn the loop wrong side out (seam allowances on the outside). With the right sides facing, center one snipped section of the bottom edge on one edge of the 11" × 11" burlap square. (Note: The square should be about ½" longer than the snipped section on either side.) Pin into place. Work around the rest of the square, aligning and pinning.

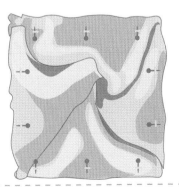

7. Sew all the way around the edges using a ½" seam allowance, backstitching before and after you turn the corner. This adds strength.

8. Trim the seam allowances to ¼" around the corners to give the square sharpness. Turn the outside basket right side out.

9. Work the bottom edges between your fingers to fully roll out the seams. Press. Stitch around the bottom edges, ⅛" from the seams.

10. Fold the remaining burlap rectangle in half with the short edges together and the right sides facing. Stitch ½" from the raw edges to make a tube. Add a second line of stitching parallel to the first to reinforce the seam.

11. Turn the tube right side out and arrange it so that the seam is at one of the folds. Press.

12. Now sew several rows of stitching across the burlap tube. This serves to flatten and reinforce the burlap divider.

Now is a good time to put everything away and call it a day, especially if time is of the essence. Take a pause. Enjoy a few minutes of meditation, breathing, a cup of tea, or, if the time is right, maybe a nice cold beer if you're so inclined. If you have time to continue, and your brain isn't frazzled by those instructions, by all means, carry on.

Part Three

This is the final part of the project and should take about an hour or so if you're working by yourself. It'll take more time if the kids are helping. It's fun to see the basket take shape and fun, too, to picture

it on your table, nicely serving as a vessel for your cloth napkins.

Steps

1. Bring the short ends of the long fabric strip together. Stitch together, ½" from the short edges.

2. Press the seam allowance open.

3. Arrange the loop so that the seam is in the center (10" from either side). Press the side folds to make creases.

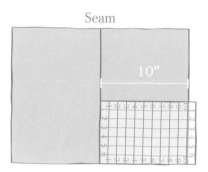

Seam

10"

4. On one of the side folds, measure up 6½" from the bottom edge and make a mark. Cut the fabric along the crease up to the mark. Repeat on the other side.

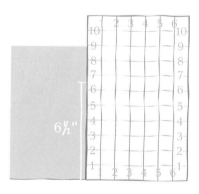

6½"

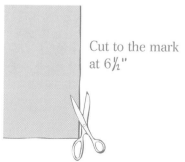

Cut to the mark at 6½"

5. Arrange the loop so that one of the slits is in line with the seam. Press the folds at the sides.

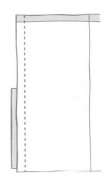

6. Rearrange the loop so that the other slit is in line with the seam. Press the folds at the sides.

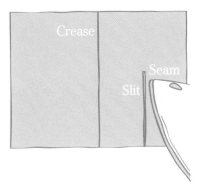

7. Make ½" snips at the folds as described in Part Two, Step 5.

8. Arrange the loop so that one of the 6½" slits is at the left folded edge. Insert the divider into the slit so that the top of the divider is at the top of the slit and the edges of the burlap stick out about ¼" on the side. Pin.

9. Stitch the divider into place, ¼" from the slit edge of the fabric. Sew from the bottom edge up to past the top of the divider and then to the top edge of the fabric, ¼" from the fold. Repeat the insertion and stitching process with the other divider end with the slit on the right folded edge.

10. Fold the top raw edge over ¼" to the wrong side. Stitch into place, ⅛" from the folded edge.

11. Attach the bottom piece as described in Part Two, Steps 6-8. Trim the seam allowance to ¼" to reduce bulk.

12. Place the fabric box inside the burlap box (wrong sides facing) and push and coax it into position. Be sure to align the side creases and get the bottom squares lined up nicely. The fabric should be several inches taller than the burlap. Do *not* fold over the top of the fabric just yet.

13. On the four side creases, pinch the edges together and sew a line of stitching about ⅛" from the fold. Stitch from the top edge to the bottom corner, and be sure to catch your fabric in the seam as well as your burlap. This serves to really stabilize the shape of your basket. Stitch around the bottom edges of the burlap basket, about ⅛" from the seam.

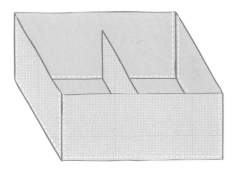

14. Now fold the top of the fabric over the top of the burlap and whip-stitch it into place all the way around the basket.

There you go. You did it! You may now serve something delicious to the entire family and not worry about messy fingers and mouths. Or catch-alls. Remember, you've been forewarned about those.

Table Runner

Table Runner

Our family dinners are not usually about the food. Sure, we like to have a nice meal, but our main objective is really to have time as a family, all together, facing each other, with nothing else to take our time. Phones are off and our attention is put to the task of just being there. Dinner time is a rare treat, to be sure, because so many other parts of our daily existence are wrapped up in activities, events, and other obligations or distractions. Gathering together is the point, and it doesn't matter whether we're having popcorn and smoothies or a fully prepared feast. You can only imagine how our kids just love our fully prepared feasts. Nary a complaint. They just eat and appreciate all the efforts that went into it all. Don't your kids?

Though we do love the evening gatherings, sometimes we get in cycles where the family dinner becomes less frequent than we'd like. We've found, though, that the rituals that are part of our meal, such as the rituals supported by a table runner like this, make it so that we can return to the dinner-time habit fully ready to dive right in no matter how long it's been since we last gathered together at the table.

Note: *We have marked our table runner with the four elements: earth, air, fire, and water. The four elements each represent an element of the things we like at family dinners. Earth is the spot to put a flower or cutting in a vase. Water holds our water pitcher. Fire is a place for a candle, which we light at the beginning of each meal and blow out after the meal is over (or sometimes during the meal if the toddler has his way). Air holds our prompts for blessings and our talking prompts, which we cover in another project in this chapter. A small chime or bell, which you might sound at the beginning of the meal, could also go here. You can, of course, mark your table runner in whatever way works for you. What are the things that are important to your family meal?*

• **Finished Measurements:** 12" W; length customized for table •

Supplies

½ yard burlap (60" width) or one large burlap coffee bag for the runner base. For runners longer than 60", purchase an additional ½ yard of burlap.

4 scraps of quilt-weight fabric larger than 7" × 12" for the fabric blocks. If purchasing fabric off the bolt, ask for ¼ yard of each.

¼ yard quilt-weight fabric for the stamped strips

Alphabet stamps with letters sized 1½" or smaller

Glue stick

Fabric paint

Paint brush

1 3-yard package of ½" double-fold bias tape for 60" runners (2 packages for longer runners). If you'd like to make your own bias tape (see instructions on page 139), you need 1 yard of fabric.

Note: *For our alphabet stamps, we used the fabric printing stamps made by Magnetic Poetry. Also, hunting for used coffee bags for this project is a great excuse to taste-test several variants of all your favorite fancy coffee drinks. Order something new, chat up your local roaster, and find out where he or she stores the empty bags. Most places are glad to share.*

Part One

With the whole family present discuss what elements are currently a regular part of your meals. A few minutes after everyone is done eating and before you clear the table is a good time for this conversation. From that list, discuss what parts you actually want as a regular element at your meals. Let everyone make suggestions from things that inspire them and discuss all ideas as a family. Put it all on the table (ha ha!) and then vote or make a decision in whatever way your family usually uses. (Rock, paper, scissors maybe?) From that discussion, you can develop your words and your design for your family's personalized table runner. If you really like our earth, air, fire, water idea, by all means, use it. Our mothers told us repeatedly that imitation is the sincerest form of flattery. We didn't always believe them. But we do now. Be sure to give yourselves plenty of time and turn off all distractions so that your conversation can be complete.

Part Two

We've broken the actual project into two parts but you can complete it in one if you have the energy, the time, and the patience.

This first part of the project involves small pieces so you do not need a huge space. A table top should suffice. Even a table top with piles of papers stacked at one end should work. Not that our table ever looks like that. In fact, if you let us know a few minutes before you come over, you will see that our table is perfectly cleaned and wiped all the time. Ask anybody.

Steps

1. Cut a 7" × 12" rectangle from each of the four scrap fabrics.

2. Cut four 3" × 12" strips from the other fabric.

3. Fold the long edges of the eight pieces of fabric over to the wrong side ½" or so. Press a nice crease that will hold until you complete the stitching steps. Use steam or starch as needed.

4. Mix the fabric paint with just a tiny bit of water in a shallow dish. A large yogurt top works well as a dish for the paint.

5. Place the smaller strips right side up on your work surface.

6. Brush each stamp with a bit of the fabric paint.

7. If you haven't stamped before, practice first on a scrap piece of fabric and then stamp your words on the small pieces of cloth. In our case we stamped Earth, Air, Fire, and Water. We made our words slightly off-center. You decide how you'd like yours to look. This is a really fun process for everyone and you can fight over . . . we mean *discuss* who gets to do what. Maybe take turns each doing a word.

8. Sing a song about the elements, which should totally drive your children nuts. If you don't know a song, find one online.

Part Three

Because you will be looking at this table runner a lot as it sits on your dining room or kitchen table, make sure you choose good materials. If you are using burlap bags for the base, find one that has a good design and good weave. Sometimes the weave is too large, which makes for difficult sewing. Some burlap bags are just perfect and are so amazingly beautiful that you can't even believe they are supposed to be considered disposable.

Steps

1. Cut a piece of burlap 12" × the desired length. (If you are using burlap off the bolt, the full 60" width is convenient. For longer runners, or runners made from burlap bags, some piecing is necessary. Simply cut 12"-wide pieces and sew them together to get the desired length. You can even plan ahead so that the seams are hidden by the fabric blocks.)

2. Use a coffee mug as a template to round off the corners (see the illustration).

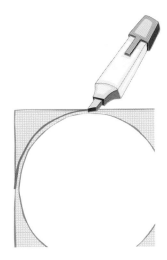

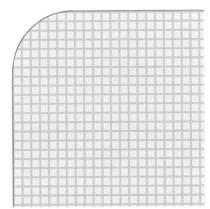

3. Apply a touch of glue from the glue stick around the edges on the wrong side of each of the blocks (this helps keep the layers together during stitching). Position your blocks on the burlap in an arrangement that pleases you. Add a few pins to hold the blocks in place and stitch them to the burlap, about ⅛" from the folded edges.

4. Position the stamped strips atop the blocks. Pin and then stitch into place about ⅛" from the folded edges.

5. Apply bias tape (see appendix).

Now look at your job chart and see whose turn it is to set the table. Whoever it is will be happy to have this new addition to the table, which makes it feel rather festive and also makes it easier to remember just what is needed and where it should go. Your helpers will just come skipping along when you call and won't complain at all about having to stop what they're doing to help with family chores. Really. It's *that* good.

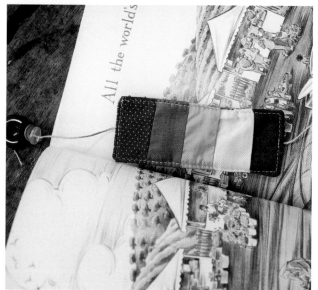

chapter 4
library time

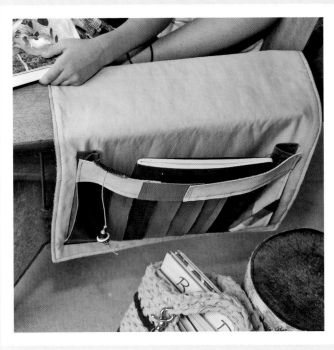

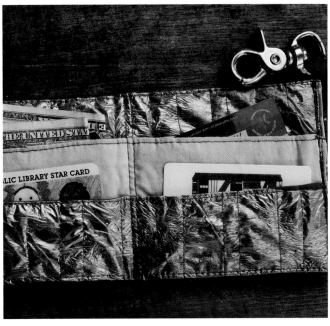

The library is a great invention. Ben Franklin is credited with the idea of a lending library, although he apparently charged a subscription fee. The ancient Romans had a system, too, of leaving scrolls in public bath houses, which were reserved for the wealthy. The free public library system started in Boston in the mid 1800s and it was surely inspired by earlier inclinations to share the richness of books. Since then, the library system has evolved into a public book-lending system that's virtually free and is available to all.

Going to the library is one of family life's great pleasures. Not only is it free, but it's ever changing. There are always new books and unknown subjects to peruse and explore. The library offers something for everyone. And the time spent browsing through the stacks can provide endless hours of ideas, inspiration, and entertainment.

In our homes everyone—from the parents to the pre-teens right down to the resident toddler—loves to read and share what they've read and learned with each other. We all love to pour over all manner of books—graphic novels, chapter books, picture books, craft books, and more.

In our own family outings to the library we have learned that "free" doesn't always mean "without cost." We have paid replacement fees for lost books that we wouldn't have purchased at a yard sale for a quarter. We have paid enough late fees to purchase practically every book we've ever checked out. And although we appreciate that the library loans us DVDs and CDs as well as books, we have paid a steep price when those said items have been abandoned in the player for weeks on end. We don't even want to think about how much it cost us when the library first went to a strictly electronic system and stopped putting those awesome rubber stamp expiration dates on the index cards in the little manila pockets.

For a long time we didn't really mind the money spent on overdue and replacement fees. We looked at the fees as our contribution to the library system's purchase and maintenance of our beloved books. One day though, while whipping out the debit card for some exorbitant lost/late/damaged book fee, we told the librarian about our theory on paying late fees. "Oh," she commented, "actually the late fees don't go to us; they just go into the city's general fund."

Believe us when we say that we love all our city services. Really and truly we do. Things like water and sewer are as important as the libraries. But the general fund? That put a different light on things altogether.

In our respective homes, with our respective broods, we called a few family meetings about our library issues. We brainstormed and strategized. We attached book receipts to the calendar and to the car dashboard and taped them to the bathroom mirror. Still the late fees persisted. It was time to get crafty as we set our sights on ways to diminish our tardy returns. Consequently we designed a few systems for ourselves, for our families, and for our borrowed books.

What we all agreed was needed was a central holding location. A regular spot for the library books to live, such as the crocheted bag in this chapter and also the arm chair caddy. A place for all our library cards was needed, too, as mom's wallet wasn't always accessible; hence the attachable library card wallet. We also needed a way to identify the books readily so that they could be spotted even laying in a pile of other random selections. And the button bookmarks were born. Truly, these projects have changed both of our families' borrowing practices. And with a swank new neighborhood library right down the street from both of us, it's all just in time.

Although we don't promise that you'll never have a late fee again, we do believe these projects will give your library books a proper place in your home and help you keep your place in those books you are reading.

So get crafting. Then get to the library and load up on a whole week's worth of tomes. What better way to relax and connect than over a fresh new stack of books!

Library Tote Bag

Library Tote Bag

The hours after we return home from the library are pure magic as everyone browses their books from his or her own comfy space. The only sound is of everyone quietly turning the pages. The challenge is keeping our books, CDs, and other library paraphernalia in one place for their timely return to the library's stacks.

After you start using this library tote bag, you'll be so organized you'll never pay another late fee again! With the bag's comfortable strap that's perfect for slinging over your shoulder, going to the library has never been easier or more eco-chic! When you return home with your bag full of books, the bag sits beautifully as a floor basket, ready to hold all your books in one place. When it's time to return for the next batch of books, just grab the bag and go!

The creation of this bag/basket has totally transformed our library visits. No more random storage places for our library materials. No more "where should I put this?" And no more scrambling on library day to find all the missing pieces. This bag carries as nicely as it sits and it's always at home on whichever floor it lives.

● **Finished Measurements:** 14" L × 6" W × 10" H ●

Supplies

Size P or Q (15–16mm) crochet hook

2 twin bed sheets, any size, each a different color (colored or patterned is best instead of plain white)

Scissors

Safety pins

Sewing thread and needle, or sewing machine

One removable stitch marker (optional)

Part One

This project, like many of ours, is yearning for adaptation. We've given you the basics of what you need to do to re-create our sample, but we expect that you'll make adjustments to the pattern to work with your home, family, needs, and style.

This basket is a bit on the small side for a true family library bag. (At least it's small for the way *we* do the library. We do the library in a big way, my friends.) But it serves nicely as a personal library bag, especially if you feel the need to limit the quantity of booty each person takes home to read.

Determine your needs based on your family members' ages and library habits. Do you want one big bag? Or are several small bags, which can be lined up with each person's stash sitting nicely in them, a better fit for you?

Part Two

This part is about making your "yarn," which takes just about as long as the crocheting part but it can give you a certain crazy satisfaction. We used two bed sheets—one a red twin flat sheet and the other a blue twin fitted sheet. If you don't have an old bed sheet that you're ready to upcycle, check out a good thrift store near you, ask a neighbor, go to a garage sale, or even look on Craigslist or some other sale site. Used bed sheets are abundant; you just have to figure out where to find them. If you have a sheet from a different project, use it! Just trim it to an even rectangle.

Steps

To make one, continuous 2"-wide strip of yarn from a sheet, you sew the sheet into a tube with the edges not perfectly matched up, then you cut around the tube in a big spiral, as follows:

1. If you have a fitted sheet, remove the elastic and open each corner seam. Trim the excess fabric to create a nice, even rectangle. Any size or dimension rectangle will do, but the smaller the rectangle, the less "yarn" you can make. If you want a bigger bag, you need more yarn.

Note: *Take a deep breath before starting the following steps. You're going to be making 2-inch-wide strips out of the sheets. The instructions might seem confusing, but they're really quite simple.*

2. Fold the sheet in half with the shorter ends together, laying one end about 2" over the other to make a tube.

3. Shift one of the edges of the sheet 2" to the right, so the ends are no longer lined up exactly. (See the illustration.)

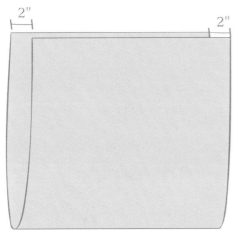

Match short ends with 2" hanging over on each edge

4. Pin the two ends together and sew along the edge of one sheet, then turn the tube inside out and sew along the edge of the other sheet. You should now have a tube of fabric with the seam offset by 2" at the edges.

5. Start at one end of the tube, where there's 2" of fabric to the side of the seam where it meets with the other end. Cut about an inch down the overhanging fabric. From that clip, tear down the length of the sheet (that is, around the tube) until you've returned to the seam where your sewing stops you from tearing further.

6. Cut through the seam where the tear meets it, which enables you to continue tearing around the tube again.

7. Continue to tear and clip at the seam until the entire sheet has been torn into one long 2"-wide strip. Feel the joy of tearing fabric. Let your children feel the joy of tearing fabric. Listen to the satisfying sound of threads popping. *Ahh*, sweet catharsis. This, my friends, is stress release of the highest order.

Clip here and start tearing

8. *Pause for the crazy laughing that will surely ensue.*

9. Wind your yarn into a ball. This is another Zen-like chore that you could keep to yourself, or you could importantly delegate it to a willing subcontractor.

Part Three

You might need more than a day to complete this project, depending on your skill level and your attention span. But we've called it Part Three because for all intents and purposes these are the final steps to completing your bag, and you can conceivably finish everything in just one day.

Before you start, know that making this bag is not rocket science and keeping it loose and simple is a sure way to make this a much more enjoyable project for the whole family. If your head has ever threatened to explode when glancing at a knitting or crochet pattern, then this pattern is for you.

Stitch Guide and Crochet Instructions

1. Slip Knot: Leaving about an 8" tail, hold the yarn in one hand and extend your pointer finger. With your other hand, wrap the yarn all the way around your finger. Push the yarn, from back to front, through the loop on your finger but don't pull it all the way through. Slip the yarn off your finger and tug on the loop you pushed through, until the knot is snug. Put the loop (the slip knot) on your hook.

2. Chain: Yarn over by wrapping the yarn over the hook from back to front, grab the yarn with the hook and draw it through the loop on your hook (now there's one loop on your hook from the chain you just made). Yarn over and draw through the loop on your hook to make as many chain stitches as you need.

3. Single Crochet: Insert your hook in the next stitch, yarn over and pull the yarn through the stitch (now there are 2 loops on your hook), yarn over and draw the yarn through both loops on your hook (now there's one loop on your hook).

Steps

1. Using a size P or Q crochet hook and referring to the Stitch Guide where needed, start with a slip knot on your hook, then chain 12 for your foundation chain. It should be about 6" long.

Note: *For the rest of the bag, we use the only crochet stitch we know. And originally we didn't even know what it's called, but now we do. We tell you this so that you realize that you too can crochet, even if you always thought it was too complicated.*

2. To create the flat oval base of your bag, take the foundation chain you just made and begin to build on it. Keeping the loop of the last stitch you made on your hook, turn back on the chain. Skipping the last two chains you made, insert your hook through the loop (any loop—just find a place to stick the hook through) of the third stitch from your hook and make a single crochet (refer to the Stitch Guide).

3. Single crochet in each stitch across the chain until you reach the first stitch of the chain (you've made 9 single crochets). You are now at one end of what will become the oval that forms the base of the bag.

4. In order to keep the bottom of the bag flat, you need to add stitches around the ends of the oval. When you stop increasing at the ends, the crocheted fabric begins to curl up, forming the sides of the bag. So you need to increase at the ends until the base of the bag is the basic size you'd like for your bag. For the bag pictured, we made the base by crocheting 5 rounds, increasing at the ends of the oval in each round.

5. So, in that last stitch of the foundation chain, make 2 single crochets—after you make one stitch, go back through the same base stitch again to make a second. On your first turn around the oval you need to add two stitches at each edge. The next time you add two more *each* to the two you added, and so on (so on subsequent rounds, you add 4 stitches to your total stitch count on each round). If you feel like your base is curling upwards at all, add a few more stitches along the sides and/or ends.

6. Now work back along the underside of the foundation chain, making 9 single crochets. When you reach the first stitch, make 2 single crochets. If you want, place a removable stitch marker in the last stitch you made to mark the end of the round so you can easily keep track of the number of rounds you work.

7. For the second round, make a single crochet in each of the next 9 stitches. Make 2 single crochets in each of the next two stitches. Now you're on the other side of the oval, so make 9 single crochets, then make 2 single crochets in each of the last 2 stitches of the round.

8. Continue making rounds like this, increasing twice (or as needed) at each end of the oval.

When the base has reached the size you'd like, stop increasing and just stitch into each existing stitch to build up the sides of the bag.

9. When you'd like to add a stripe, stop, cut your "yarn," leaving about 6" of tail, and tie the tail securely to a different color of "yarn" (which is from your second sheet), and keep on keepin' on. You can tuck the little knots where you tie your yarn together to the inside of the bag to keep the appearance neat. After the initial nine rounds of red yarn, we switched to the blue yarn and made five more rounds. Then we switched back to the red and made one more round. For the top of the bag before the handle, we switched back to blue and made one round.

10. When your bag is as tall as you'd like and you want to add handles, crochet to the point on one side of the bag where you want the handle to start. Make a chain (in the same way you made a chain at the beginning) that's about the length of the handle you want (ours is made up of 15 chains). Then skip the section of the bag that's the width you want the handle to be (we skipped 9 stitches). Insert your hook in the next stitch after the ones you're skipping, and crochet around until you get to where you want the handle to be on the other side of the bag, trying to keep it as symmetrical as possible. Repeat for the second handle.

11. Finally, crochet one more round all the way around the top of the bag and the handle chains, which makes the handles thicker and stronger.

12. When you are finished, cut the yarn 8" from the last stitch and pull it through the loop from the last stitch to fasten it off. Then weave the loose end back through a few stitches to secure it.

This bag/basket is super sturdy and at the same time super flexible and easy to tote and toss around. You will love having this serve as a "home" for all your incoming library items and a sweet accessory to your family's living/reading quarters. What are you going to read next?

Library Card Wallet

Library Card Wallet

We came up with this idea because too often it felt like one or another library card was scattered to the wind, never to be found again. Sometimes one of our library cards has been sent through the laundry and washed and dried to an illegible state. Then there are the times we arrived at the library to check out books only to realize that we a) had no card with us or b) had no money to pay the fine or c) couldn't find our receipt to let us know when the books we had borrowed needed to be returned.

This simple little design, with clip included, has changed all that. The library card wallet now serves as a clearinghouse for all the aforementioned items. All the family's cards have a spot in the wallet along with a few bucks for fines. The wallet is also where we store our receipt so that we know where to look for that otherwise elusive due date. Problems solved, easy as can be. We'd like to say we'll never have another late fee again, but we don't want to push our luck. We have, however, definitely reduced the number of fines we pay, and we also manage to avoid the pre-library visit, "where-are-our-library-cards?" scramble.

● **Finished Measurements:** 9" × 4" wallet ●

Supplies

2 colors of cotton quilt-weight fabric, 1 fat quarter each (ask for ⅜ of a yard if buying fabric off the bolt).

Note: *You can use scraps of bed sheets or other cottons. That's what we used for the sample shown in the photo.*

1 metal clip or carabineer

Note: *A cast-off purse or pack is a good place to find a metal clip or carabineer to use for this project.*

1 button

1 elastic hair band or other small piece of elastic

2 thin plastic bags of the grocery store variety

2 pieces of large paper (such as parchment paper, wax paper, or butcher paper), for use in fusing your plastic bags

Note: *As an alternative to fusing plastic bags, you can use a light, flexible material such as plastic tarp. You need a piece that is at least 10" × 12".*

Part One

This part of the project is kind of fun because you are actually creating crafting material out of something you have seen practically every day of your life. This is true upcycling: taking something that most likely will be disposed of, making it stronger, and using it for your project. It's called "fusing plastic," and you do it with an iron and a couple of plastic bags.

Steps

1. Set the iron on a medium temperature.

Note: *You may need to do a bit of experimenting to determine the ideal fusing conditions. If the iron is too hot, the plastic will melt and tear. If the iron is too cool, the layers will not stick together.*

2. Cut the handles and bottom seam off your plastic bags and then open the bags to make loops.

3. If your bags have printing on them, turn them inside out so that the ink from the printing doesn't stick to the paper you'll be ironing the plastic between.

4. For best results, do your fusing on a flat, non-meltable surface (a large wooden cutting board works great). Cut a piece of paper that is larger than your bags and lay it out on your ironing surface. Center and stack the looped bags atop the paper. You should have four layers of plastic in total. Cut a second piece of paper and place it on top of the bag stack. Make sure that your paper is larger than your plastic bags. When you iron, the plastic should always be in the middle of the paper.

5. Starting in the center of the sandwich, iron a very small section for approximately 10–15 seconds. Keep the iron moving in a circular fashion to prevent iron marks. After a brief cooling period, check your plastic. See if it looks evenly fused together. If there are large bubbles or areas that look unfused, place the plastic back in the paper or wax paper sandwich and iron a bit more, being careful not to over-iron already fused areas, as this can begin to melt the plastic. Working out from the center, fuse the bags together in small sections.

6. Cut a 10" × 12" piece of each of the two quilt-weight cottons.

7. Trim your fused plastic (or plastic material) to 10" × 12".

8. Place your fused plastic sheet atop the piece of cotton that you'd like to show through the plastic on the outside of the wallet, with the "right" sides of both pieces facing up. Run several lines of stitching parallel to one another up and down the two pieces in order to "quilt" them together. You can measure these lines and space them very evenly, or stitch in a random fashion for a crazy quilt look. (You can consider these two pieces your "quilted" piece.)

9. Lay your quilted piece atop your other piece of cotton, right sides together, and pin them. Starting in the middle of one long side, stitch all the way around the pieces ½" from the edges, making sure to leave a 2"–3" opening for turning. Trim the seam allowance around the corners.

10. Turn the piece right side out, so the right side of the cotton fabric is showing on one side, and the stitched plastic side is showing on the other. Work the edges between your fingers to fully turn out the seams. Tuck the seam allowance into place at the opening. Topstitch all the way around, ⅛" from the edges.

11. Cut a 1" × 3" piece of quilt-weight cotton for the loop. Fold the piece in half lengthwise with the good sides facing and stitch around two of the three open edges with a ¼" seam allowance, leaving one end open.

12. Turn the small piece right side out and top stitch down both long sides.

Part Two

This next part is fun and comes from an idea we saw for making origami wallets out of paper. We modified it quite a bit, but the idea is still inspired by origami. Play around with this a bit by trying different sized folds. See what works for you.

These steps are really good to do with kids because all the stitches are straight and simple.

Steps

1. Place your fabric rectangle flat on your work surface with the quilted side facing up.

2. Fold down the top short edge approximately 2" (quilted sides facing). Stitch along the sides of the fold, about ⅛" from the edges.

3. Flip your project over to the fabric side and then fold the top over again (fabric sides facing) approximately 3½". With the project in the same position, fold up the bottom of the project approximately 2". (See the illustration.)

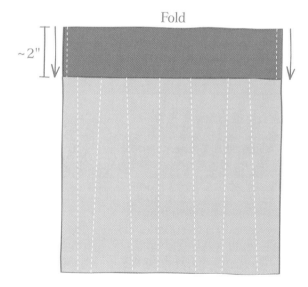

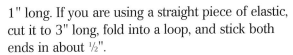

Fold

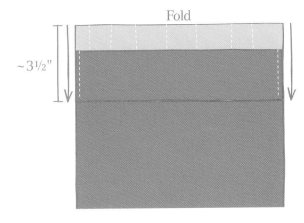

~ 3½"

Fold

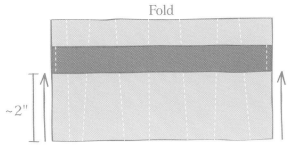

~ 2"

1" long. If you are using a straight piece of elastic, cut it to 3" long, fold into a loop, and stick both ends in about ½".

6. Stitch all the way around the perimeter of your wallet, making sure to double stitch over the area where your cotton loop and your elastic are inserted.

7. Fold the wallet in half widthwise and align the edges. Squeeze the fold to make a visible crease (if the crease is hard to see, mark the position with a washable marker). Run two lines of stitches from the top to the bottom on either side of the crease. (See the illustration.)

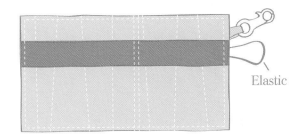

Elastic

4. In the top corner of the fold, stick one end of your small flat piece of cotton. Now, place your metal clip or carabineer on top of the cotton and fold the cotton in half so you can tuck the other end of the cotton under the wallet fabric to create a loop.

5. Insert the elastic into the side of the wallet about 1" below the loop. If you are using a hair band, arrange it so that the exposed loop is about

8. Attach the button to the middle of the outside of the wallet directly across from the elastic loop (see page 139 for button sewing instruction). Take care to not stitch through the inner pocket layers.

That's it.

Part Three

This part is easiest of all. The only thing you need to do is gather up all your library cards wherever they may be. Find a few bucks to stick in your wallet. And either head to the library for a few family books or sit around and read together. Being able to sit next to your kids when each of you is immersed in a good book is truly one of the most satisfying parenting moments. Take note of it. Stick it in your list of mental appreciations. And pause every now and again to talk about what you're reading.

Arm Chair Caddy

Arm Chair Caddy

If you've made the library tote bag, you already have a place to store the books that have just come from or are ready to go back to the library. But what do you do with the books that are currently being read? You need to keep your current reads accessible so that you can easily find them when the desire strikes. (Because, as any parent knows, the window of opportunity or inspiration must be seized whenever it presents itself.) Having this Arm Chair Caddy for your current reading pleasures makes it so that you spend less time searching and more time reading. The caddy features two pockets—one large, heavy-weight pocket for big books or a stack of magazines, and a lighter-weight divided pocket for smaller books and/or reading accessories such as glasses and bookmarks.

● **Finished Measurements:** 29" × 15" ●

Supplies

- ½ yard (or at least a 30" × 16" rectangle) medium-weight fabric for the exterior of the caddy base.

- ½ yard (or at least a 30" × 16" rectangle) home décor fabric for the underside of the caddy base

- ¼ yard non-fraying medium- to heavy-weight material (or at least a 9" × 13" rectangle) for the outside pocket, OR an array of heavy-weight scraps; possibilities include vinyl, suede, or thick wool felt

- ¼ yard of medium-weight fabric (or at least enough for two 4" × 9½" rectangles) for the sides of the heavy-weight pocket

- ⅓ yard light- to medium-weight fabric (or at least enough scrap for a 18" × 10½" rectangle) for the thinner divided pocket

- Coordinating thread

- Pointy object, such as a point turner or knitting needle

- Upholstery needle

Part One

For this part just examine your family's rhythm of reading. Where do you spend most of your reading time? Does that work for you? In the place you spend a lot of your reading time, what chair would be ideally suited for holding a caddy like this one? After you determine the location, you need to figure out the shape of the chosen couch or chair. We made ours to fit specifically over a fat arm of a chair. Measure the width of your chair. Perhaps yours is fat (if so, add a couple inches to the length of the caddy base) or narrow (if so, shorten your caddy base by 2"–4") or maybe it's wood instead of cloth (if so you may want to be more mindful of finding a non-slip backing fabric for your caddy base). Take a look. Take some measurements, too, and adjust your project accordingly. It's definitely not an exact science and there is some wiggle room for sure.

After you have finished figuring and writing down the measurements, get out your family's current reading pleasure, be it chapter book or poetry, instructional guide or atlas. Sit together and share in the joy of reading. If you are all currently reading something different, perhaps you could take turns reading sections out loud to each other. Practicing reading aloud and practicing listening are about the two most important life skills ever. Clear communication is the key to familial harmony!

Part Two

This part of the project is about fabric choice, acquisition, and cutting. For this project, when considering the fabric for the back of the caddy, try to find a fabric that will "grip" the fabric of your couch or chair. We found a piece of home décor fabric that was particularly knobby, which is great for holding the fabric in place when weighted down with a few books. Burlap or corduroy are good choices, too.

For our heavy-weight pocket, we used fabric samples from a fabric sample book. The upholsterer from whom we acquired these literally threw these into our lap. He was relieved that he had found someone to use these pieces that would have ended up in the trash otherwise.

Steps

1. Check your local phone book and find an upholsterer near you. Other options are auto refurbishers, restaurant suppliers, or interior designers. All of these businesses use sample books and many of these sample books are changed out seasonally as new fabric lines become available.

Spend the morning calling around. When you find a contact who has an outdated fabric sample book, that person will be *more* than happy to have you come by and pick it up. In addition to the sample books, many upholsterers have extra swaths of cloth that are plenty big for your needs but are too small for any of their projects. The upholsterer might need a head's up or they might just have some pieces readily available for pick up. This is a good task for an older child who can benefit from the practice of calling businesses and asking for what they need.

2. Cut 30" × 16" rectangles from both the caddy exterior (medium-weight) and caddy underside (home décor) fabrics.

3. Cut a 13" × 9" piece of the non-fraying fabric. This is your heavy-weight pocket front.

Note: *We assembled our 13" × 9" piece of fabric from smaller pieces. If you do this as well, layer and stitch together your scraps and then cut the larger piece to 13" × 9". This is a great kid project because even if it isn't pieced together exactly straight, you can cut it straight later. A child can even do it in a crazy assemblage, letting their desire for chaos reign!*

4. Cut two 4" × 9½" pieces of the medium-weight fabric for your pocket sides.

5. Cut an 18" × 10½" piece of lighter-weight fabric for the divided pocket.

Part Three

Time to sew. This is the most time-consuming part of the project, not counting driving around town to pick up materials. Like some of the other projects, this project includes lots of small steps that are easy for kids to do. There is some room for error as well and, even more importantly, there is room for a bit of creative expression. For creative inspiration you might want to get out some of your favorite books and have them waiting so that they can be inserted in the caddy as soon as it is finished.

Steps

1. Place the caddy interior and exterior pieces together with the right sides facing. Using a ½" seam allowance, sew around all four edges, leaving a 2"–3" opening for turning.

2. Clip the corners carefully, making sure not to clip your seam. Turn the piece right side out, using a knitting needle or some other pointy object to make sure the corners are turned all the way out. Turn the edges of the opening into place and pin and press. Topstitch all the way around the caddy base, ⅛" from the edges.

3. For each of the two 4" × 9½" side pocket pieces: Fold the long edges ¼" to the wrong side and press.

4. Fold the top short edge ½", press, and stitch into place ¼" from the fold.

5. Fold each rectangle in half lengthwise, right side facing in. Press to make a sharp crease.

6. Align the long, folded edge of one of your side pieces with the short cut edge of your heavy-weight pocket front with the wrong sides together. Pin and stitch together, ⅛" from the aligned edges. (See the illustration.)

7. Repeat Step 6 for the second side piece.

8. After both pocket sides are stitched to your pocket front, place the heavy-weight pocket on the caddy base, centering it approximately 1" from the bottom of the caddy base.

9. Arrange the sides so that the unstitched folds are in line with the side edges of the pocket front. Pin the folded edges of the sides (but not the front) to the caddy base. Stitch into place, ⅛" from the edges.

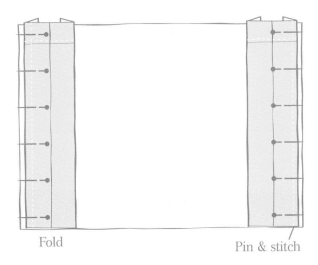

Fold   Pin & stitch

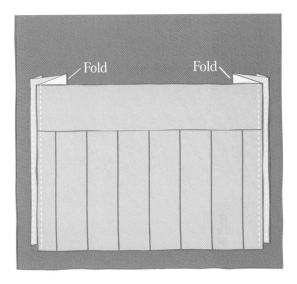

10. Refold the pocket sides so that they are beneath the pocket front. Stich into place, ¼" from the bottom edge of the pocket front.

Note: *Depending on the thickness of your material, it might be necessary to use a heavy duty upholstery needle in your machine.*

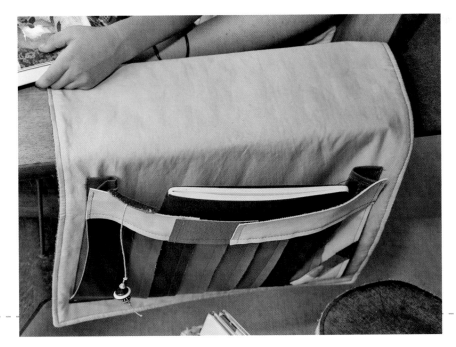

11. Fold all of the edges of the light-weight fabric ¼" and press. Make a second 1¼" fold in the top long edge of the fabric. Stitch into place, ⅛" from the first folded edges.

12. Fold both of the short side edges to the wrong side, 2" from the initial fold. Edge stitch ⅛" from both of these two new folds to permanently set them in place.

13. Place the pocket piece with the wrong side facing up. For each side, bring the first folded edge over to meet the second folded edge. Press to make a pleat.

14. Pin the pocket sides to the caddy base and stitch together as described in Step 9. After the sides are stitched down, edge stitch the bottom of the pocket down, ⅛" from the edge.

15. Split the pocket by stitching a seam down the middle of the pocket, making sure to backstitch at the top and bottom.

Note: *We chose to add a little color by taking some scraps from the strips we sewed for the bookmarks, pressing both sides in, and stitching them down to the corners of our pockets. You can add anything you want to embellish your caddy. Maybe an appliqué? Or a patch won in a reading contest? Use any random embellishment you like.*

Now you're finished. Lay this caddy over the arm of your chair, load it up with everyone's current favorite book, and settle on in for an afternoon family read-a-thon.

Button Bookmarks

Button Bookmarks

The problem in our house is that we have so many books that sometimes the library books get mixed in with our own. We created these jingly-jangly bookmarks to help make sure our library books never get lost in the regular book shelf shuffle. They are long enough on each end to catch our eye and therefore serve as a visual reminder that this book shouldn't be shelved!

This project is simple and definitely has lots of room for creative interpretation. For that reason this is a great project on which the kiddos can lead a little bit. Selecting the buttons and fabrics and string are all things that can be done without any parental input whatsoever.

These bookmarks make great gifts, too. Because they are so simple, making them and giving them in abundance is very satisfying. So make a bunch, keep them in reserve and give them out at your next party or with a book for a perfect birthday gift.

• **Finished Measurements:** Five 5¼" × 2" bookmarks •

Supplies

5 different fabric scraps that are at least 2" × 12½". You can use fat quarters, or, if purchasing yardage off the bolt, ask for ⅛ yard cuts.

4'–5' of hemp twine (or other strong string)

Small scraps of home décor fabric totaling approximately ¼ yard

Various buttons, baubles, and beads

Part One

This is such a fun project you'll want to make oodles and oodles of bookmarks. Part One is just about making lists of all the readers you know who might want a bookmark like this. Grandma, cousins, aunts, uncles, and friends galore. How many people are on your list? How many bookmarks do you think you could make in a day? We decided that we could easily make five bookmarks.

Part Two

Assemble all your fabric options and determine which ones go together. Do you want a rainbow? Crazy mixed-up patterns? What kind of scraps do you have on hand? Play around with combining different fabrics. Talk with the kids about contrasting patterns, colors, and so on. What appeals to you? What appeals to them? This is a fun time to play, play, play while discussing the idea that there is no right way because we all like different things.

Steps

1. Cut five 1¾" × 12½" strips of scrap fabric.
2. Cut 10 6"-long pieces of hemp twine.
3. Cut five 2½" × 6¼" pieces of home décor fabric.

Part Three

You can either all work together toward a collective project, or, depending on the ages of the kids, you can each work on your own. If you have a small group of kids, a fun way to do this is for each kid to work on his or her own bookmark. At the end of the project, everyone can trade bookmarks with each other.

Steps

1. With the right sides facing, sew the five scrap fabric strips together along the long edges, creating one large stripwork rectangle that is 12½" × approximately 6¼". Press the seam allowances open.

2. Cut this rectangle into five pieces measuring 2½" × 6¼".

3. On each short side of the home décor fabric, center a length of twine, leaving about ¼" tail hanging over the edge. Stitch into place about ⅛" from the edge, backstitching once or twice to make sure the twine is caught by the stitches.

4. Roll the twine into a spiral and pin it to the fabric in order to keep it from getting in the way in the next step. (See the illustration.)

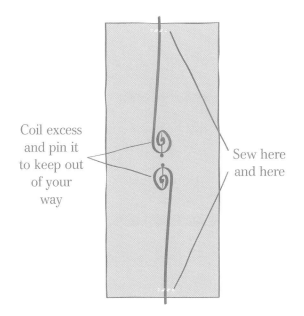

Coil excess and pin it to keep out of your way

Sew here and here

5. With the right sides together, pin the pieced fabric strip to the home décor fabric piece. Make sure all parts of the twine are tucked inside.

6. Starting near the middle of one of the longer sides of the rectangle, sew the two pieces together, ¼" from the edges, stopping about 2" from where you started so that you can turn it right side out.

7. Insert your fingers into the two sewn-together pieces and remove the pins that are holding the twine.

8. Clip the corners of the rectangle, being careful not to clip your stitching and then carefully turn it right side out.

9. Fold under the raw edges at 2" and press. Make sure the edges of the opening are even with the side of the bookmark. Topstitch all the way around the bookmark, backstitching once or twice when you are going over the twine (for added security).

10. Tie a knot in each piece of twine about 1½" from the exposed end. Your buttons and baubles are going to rest against this knot. Then thread on your buttons and beads however you'd like! See the project photo if you need help with this.

11. After the buttons and beads are added, tie a final knot to hold them in place.

That's it! It's as simple as can be. Put a bookmark in each of your library books with the buttons sticking out each end. Give a bookmark to your friends. These are too sweet and simple to keep to yourself. How many more do you want to make?

chapter 5

into the woods

We love the outdoors. We love hiking and camping and climbing trees and hanging out under the open sky on just about any kind of day. We have come to realize that when we're outside we are definitely having some of our best family time. Perhaps it is because the outdoors gives us the space we need. Or maybe it's because of the replenishing oxygen and vitamin D we get from the air and the sun. Then again, it just might be that when we're outside, family life is less messy and noisy, which makes it more spacious and relaxing, too.

One of the many beautiful things about outdoor time is that it is something everyone in our families loves—parents and kids alike. In the outdoors we can all find something that satisfies our bodies, minds, and spirits on every end of the spectrum. Whether we need to daydream on a blanket in a field or climb high in a tree or run madly down a trail, the outdoors can meet our needs when it's time for a break from the madding crowd. Sometimes we can even find inspiration for ways to bring a little bit of the outdoors into our everyday indoor worlds.

For our families, getting outdoors doesn't have to mean going far. We don't have to strap on the backpack to go in search of wilderness or other vast open spaces. We can find nature in our own backyards, in the middle of a city park, or in the inadvertent wilderness preserves that are created in abandoned and forgotten chunks of property. No matter where we are, when we are outside we can find adventure, exploration, rest, or the breath of fresh air we need to keep family life sane.

To set ourselves up for success, and to inspire our kids toward following their natural desire for the outdoors, we need to be prepared as we approach our outdoor excursions. We have rituals for heading outdoors, and we have some tools to help everyone find what they need. We created the projects in this chapter to help our families find inspiration for more walks in the woods. We wanted our time outdoors to be exciting, easy, safe, and accessible, too, because when we find the inspiration to get outdoors, we want to be able to spend our time enjoying ourselves and exploring our surroundings so that we can be recharged and inspired to tackle the rest of life.

Water-Bottle Holster

Water-Bottle Holster

If you have ever hiked with children, you know of the need for both water and snacks to keep bodies motivated and spirits willing. Without either one, the effort to continue just proves to be too much. Energy levels falter and whining dominates what is supposed to be a fun outing. This little water-bottle holster helps keep your crew effortlessly hydrated all hike long. And the kids will start out the hike feeling like they can tackle anything as long as they have this holster fastened on their backs.

If you have ever hiked with children, you also know of the need for everyone to tote his or her own equipment. One reason is that it makes the hike easier if the kids can satisfy their bodily needs without asking for permission or assistance. A second reason is that sharing a water bottle with a kid isn't always the most savory thing in the world. With this great belt, you can stop being a pack mule and stop worrying about backwash, too.

• **Finished Measurements:** 21" × 7" with adjustable belt •

Supplies

Old wetsuit or a 12" × 21" sheet of neoprene (see lunch tote project for buying recommendations). Another non-fray heavy-weight material such as marine vinyl may be substituted.

¼ yard polyester knit fabric with a one-way stretch (we used reclaimed athletic "tech" tees)

Fabric pencil or other light-colored pencil

1"-wide nylon webbing, approximately 45"

Plastic buckle

T-pins

Note: *You can recycle the nylon webbing from an old suitcase or other type of bag. Plastic buckles are on a lot of different items: old pants, bike helmets, and suitcases.*

Part One

The first part is about cutting, so you won't need your sewing machine just yet. Neoprene (or vinyl) is amazingly easy and satisfying to cut, and it's way easier for kids to cut than fabric. As you're tracing and cutting, talk about the different materials and why they are easier or more difficult to work with than other materials you've used in the past.

Steps

1. Cut a 50" × 2½" strip from the knit fabric. If you are using reclaimed tees, you might need to do some piecing.

2. Cut a 2½" × 10½" rectangle from the knit for an embellishment strip for the pocket (optional).

3. Use the fabric pencil to trace the water-bottle holster pattern from page 142 onto the heavy-weight material.

4. Trace the pattern for the bottom of the water-bottle holster from page 142 onto the heavy-weight material.

5. Trace the belt pattern from page 142 onto the heavy-weight material.

6. Cut the traced pieces from the heavy-weight material.

7. If it's not already trimmed to size, cut the nylon webbing to 45".

Parts Two and Three

Spend some time with your kids examining our sample photo closely to give them a vision of what you are making. This is one project where the photograph really helps to make sense of all the different pieces and "units" that are joined together.

Take note also that sewing heavy-weight fabric is a slower process than sewing lighter fabrics. Take your time, and don't cram the fabric. Anytime you have an option on which side to sew to, sewing the matte side is easier than sewing the glossy side.

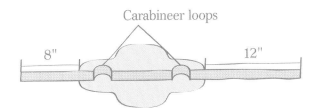

Carabineer loops

8"   12"

Steps

1. Align the right side of the strip with the outer edge of the belt piece on the wrong side. Starting 2" from the end of the strip, stitch ½" from the edges, aligning as you go. When you reach a corner, lift the presser foot, pivot, and realign. Stop stitching about 2" from the front strip end. Trim the strip so that the back end overlaps the front end by about ¼". Stretch the ends over to meet, right sides facing, and stitch together ¼" from the aligned edges. Align the loose edges of the joined strip with back edge and stitch into place (Note: If there seems to be too much strip fabric, stitch a bit further in from the short edges).

2. Flip the belt piece over to the right side and pull the strip up. Fold the strip so that the raw edge is in line with the top edge of the pouch piece. Make a second fold over to the front so that the first folded edge covers up the stitching. At the corners, make neat little pleats. Edge stitch into place, ⅛" from the first folded edge.

3. If you're using the 2½" × 10½" piece of knit for a stripe embellishment, fold in half lengthwise, right sides facing. Stitch ¼" from the long edges. Turn right side out and press.

4. Sew the strip to the front of the water-bottle holster, ⅛" from both of the long edges.

5. Position the webbing across the middle of the neoprene belt back leaving an 8" overhang on one end and a 12" overhang on the other. Create loops for a carabineer or clips on both sides of the webbing by pinning the webbing in place first and leaving a bit of slack where you want your loops to be (just make sure they are near the narrow ends of the belt so they don't get in the way of the holster). Then when you're sewing the webbing down just stitch edge to edge on either side of the loop, leaving the top open. Stitch the webbing down on the top and bottom edges. (See the illustration.)

6. With the wrong sides facing, arrange the bottom of the water-bottle holster onto the holster itself, leaving 1½" on either side of the bottom so that you can stitch the holster to the belt back in Step 7. (See the illustration.) Pin into place. Stitch together, ⅛" from the aligned edges.

Note: *Neoprene can be a little tricky to pin, but if you're using the T-pins suggested in the Supplies list you'll find it more manageable than using regular straight pins.*

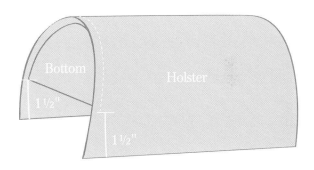

Bottom

Holster

1½"

1½"

7. Pin the bottle holster in the center of the belt back. The 1½" flaps on either side of the holster bottom should lie flat against the belt back.

8. Stitch the holster to the belt back. Reinforce your stitching by stitching a second line ¼" from your first line of stitching. (See the illustration.)

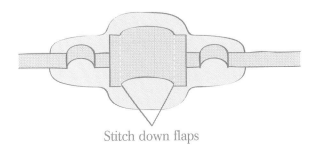

Stitch down flaps

9. Attach the buckle. Insert one end of the nylon webbing into the female piece of the buckle and pull through 2". Stitch the edge of the webbing down. Insert the other end of the webbing into the male buckle piece and pull through. This is the slide release piece, so you won't need to stitch the end of the webbing down.

10. Try the belt on its intended user. If it's too big, you can rip the stitches holding the female buckle piece in place, trim the webbing, and re-sew.

Your project is complete except for one thing, your water bottle! Find a water bottle in the house that you can refill and stuff in your belt. Try it on for size.

What else do you want to attach to your belt? A compass perhaps? Or a flashlight? Or maybe a camera to capture some shots of the animals, bugs, and plants you see? Now that your belt is sized and rigged, load it up and head outside for a practice walk around the n'hood. How's that feel? Talk about all the things you see outside, how your family feels when you're outside versus when you're inside, and how it feels when you're nourished and hydrated as opposed to not.

Lunch Tote

Lunch Tote

Out on the trail you're all going to need food in order to keep the spirits high and the energy levels raised. When everyone totes his or her own snacks, the chance for a happy and sustainable family outing just seems far more doable.

The design of this tote ensures that your food is close at hand, easy to carry, and protected from the bumps and knocks of hiking the trail. The flexible, heavy-weight fabric makes the tote comfortable to carry, and your food even stays somewhat insulated until lunch time arrives. You can attach the utility roll and nature pouch from the next project to the shoulder strap so that you have a convenient place to carry your money or other small essentials. Because this tote also has room for a few treats and treasures brought from home or picked up along the way, this bag serves as a Sherpa in its own right.

• **Finished Measurements:** 27" × 10" (including the shoulder strap) •

Supplies

½ yard of polyester knit fabric with a one-way stretch. We used a couple of athletic tees we found at the thrift store.

A heavy-duty, non-fray synthetic material. We used neoprene from an old wetsuit. Neoprene can be purchased by the sheet as well. (Look for 2 linear feet of 3mm smooth, raw black neoprene. You can upgrade to different thicknesses and colors of neoprene if you choose, but the 3mm option is the closest to what is used for the construction of an average wetsuit.) Other durable materials (such as marine vinyl) can be used in place of neoprene.

Fabric pencil or other light-colored pencil

9" of 2"-wide hook and loop tape (you'll only be using the loop part of the tape for this project, but you'll need the hook piece for the nature pouch and utility roll project).

Note: Two 9" lengths of 1"-wide hook and loop tape may be substituted.

4" of 1"-wide hook and loop tape for the pouch mouth closures.

Note: *If you are repurposing an old wetsuit we recommend giving it a good wash before cutting. You can buy special wetsuit shampoo or deodorizers. There are some environmentally safe neoprene deodorizers on the market that don't use soaps but rather use live bacteria that eat the organisms that cause odors. These can be ordered online or purchased at a local dive shop.*

Part One

If you take a good look at the photos before you get started, you will see how all the different pieces go together. Talk to the kids about visually deconstructing a piece so that they can see how the final project is a sum of smaller, more achievable parts. Let the kids practice cutting small pieces of the heavy-duty material. Show the kids how neither this material nor knit fabric unravel when cut.

Steps

1. Use the fabric pencil to trace the pattern on page 143 for the bag front pouch onto the heavy-weight material. Cut out the piece.

2. Use the pattern on page 143 to trace the strap/back piece (one piece) on the heavy-weight material and cut out the piece. This piece is cut on the fold. When we made ours out of the used wetsuit, we placed the pattern piece along the side edge of the suit. If you're using new material, you need to fold it over before you trace and cut this pattern piece.

3. Use the patterns on page 143 to trace the bag bottom pouch piece on the heavy-weight material and cut out the pieces.

4. Cut a 3¼" × 5½" rectangle from the knit fabric. This piece makes a tiny pocket for your lunch tote.

5. Use the pattern on page 143 to cut the front pocket piece (which is the same as is used for the front heavy-weight pouch piece) from knit fabric.

6. Cut two 2" pieces from your 1"-wide hook and loop tape (2 hooks, 2 loops).

7. Cut 2½"-wide strips from the knit fabric. You most likely need to cut several 2½"-wide strips and then piece them together to give you

    a. 62" to go around the outside of the bag and strap

    b. 46" to go around the inside of the strap

    c. 23" to go around the outside of the bag front

    d. 10" to go on the top of the bag front piece

Note: The strips should be cut with the long edges parallel to the direction of the stretch. On a shirt, you cut parallel to the bottom hem. For cut fabric, you need to give a tug to determine the direction of the stretch (usually it is perpendicular to the selvage edge). The 62" and 46" strips are cut a bit longer than needed so that you can trim to get just the right fit.

Parts Two and Three

You can complete this project in one day or you can stretch it over two days. Just make sure to allow yourself time and space to work with the materials.

These materials are very different than woven fabrics, and although they make the cutting much more forgiving, the stitching can get a bit tricky. Play around with some scrap pieces by cutting spirals, straight lines, and so on. Also practice stitching with these materials. Perhaps whip out a little sample pouch or just practice sewing the two materials together. The slipperiness can take a bit of patience and concentration, too. You might need to adjust your stitch length or use a heavy-duty needle for the best results. Although it might make you a little nutty, the finished product is tactilely and functionally satisfying.

Steps

1. Fold the tiny pocket piece in half widthwise, right sides facing in to make a 3¼" × 2¾" double-thickness rectangle.

2. The folded edge is the top edge of your pocket. Stitch the layers together, ¼" from the side and bottom edges. Leave a 1" opening in the center of the bottom edge for turning.

3. Trim the seam allowance at the corners. Turn the pocket right side out, tuck in the opening edges, and press. If desired, you can topstitch ½" from the folded edge to add detail to the pocket.

4. Fold the top of the front knit pocket 1" to the wrong side and press. Make a second 1" fold then stitch into place, ¼" from the first folded edge.

5. Center the tiny pocket on the front of the front knit pocket and pin it in place. Stitch along the sides and bottom of the tiny pocket to secure it to the medium pocket. Backstitch at the beginning and end of your seams. Make sure you don't sew the pocket shut along the top!

6. Decide how you want to subdivide your front knit pocket and draw lines with a washable marker.

7. Pin the front knit pocket to the front of the bag front piece and stitch it along the sides and the bottom to secure, using a ⅛" seam allowance. Sew over the markings you made in Step 6, being sure to backstitch at the beginning and end of the stitching.

8. Align the 10" strip with the top edge of the pouch piece on the wrong side. Stitch ½" from the aligned edges. Flip the pouch piece over to the right side and pull the strip up. Fold the strip so that the raw edge is in line with the top edge of the pouch piece. Make a second fold over to the front so that the first folded edge covers up the stitching and then edge stitch into place, ⅛" from the first folded edge.

9. Working on the wrong side of the pouch piece, position a 1" × 2" piece of hook tape 2" from the side edge, just below the sewn strip (see the illustration). Stitch into place.

12. Center the bag bottom piece on the pouch piece as shown in the diagram. The wrong side of the bag bottom should be facing the wrong side of the pouch piece. Pin the layers together in the center and then pin along the edges all the way up to the top edges. Note: You will have small "dog" ears at the top of the pouch (see the illustration). Stitch together, ⅜" from the aligned edges.

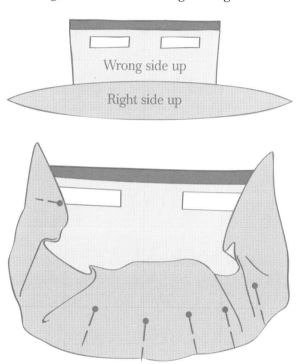

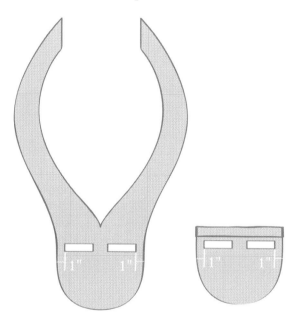

10. Repeat Step 9 to add hook tape 2" from the other edge.

11. Determine where the loop tape strips need to line up on the right side of the back of the bag so that they stick to the hook strips on the pouch front. The easiest way to do this is to place the pouch piece on the backing piece, and fold the top edge back at the bottom of the tape strips. Mark the location just above this fold and then sew the loop tape to the right side of the back of the bag. Before proceeding, make sure you can stick your pouch piece on your back piece and the edges align.

13. Now you're going to cover the seam that attaches the bag front to the bag bottom with your 20" knit strip. Beginning at either edge at the tip of a "dog ear," place the front of your knit strip facing the right side of the bag bottom. Starting at the top corner of the pouch piece, stitch ½" from the aligned edges. Stretch the strip ever so slightly as you go for a tighter binding. Stop stitching when you reach the other top corner of the pouch piece. The strip will be folded over the pouch piece as described in Step 8, except this time you fold as you stitch. You also need to fold and stitch the portions of the strip that extend beyond the top edges of the pouch so that they encase the dog ears.

Note: *If you are planning to use two days to complete the project, this is a good stopping point. Otherwise, move forward.*

14. Center the other edge of the bag bottom onto the bag back/straps piece with the wrong side of the bottom facing the right side of the back. The hook and loop tape pieces should stick together at this point. Pin together along the edges. Fold the strip tops/dog ears over and off the edge (see the illustration). Stitch together, ³⁄₈" from the aligned edges, making sure to catch the dog ears in the stitching.

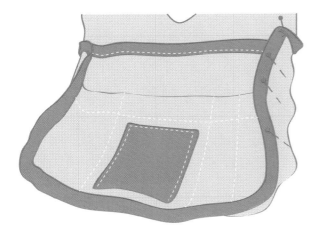

15. Fold the back piece in half lengthwise with the right sides facing and stitch together, ½" from the short shoulder edges.

16. Open the seam you've just created and run a stitch down each side of the opened seam.

17. The next step is to stitch the 62" strip all the way around the outside edge of the strap and the bag as described in the previous steps. Attach the strip first to the back with the right side of the strip facing the wrong side of the heavy-weight material. Because you're closing a circle, you need to leave a 2" flap unsewn at the start of where you attach the bias (the bottom of the bag is a good place to start). Then when you come to the end of your strip, you leave another 2" flap unsewn. Simply trim the end of the strip so that the back end overlaps the front end by about ¼". Stretch the ends over to meet, right sides facing, and stitch together ¼" from the aligned edges. Align the loose edges of the joined strip with the back edge and stitch into place. (Note: If there seems to be too much strip fabric, stitch a bit further in from the short edges.) Fold and stitch as described in the previous steps. Make sure the strip wraps around and hides the dog ears from the pouch. You might need to trim these a bit to get a smooth result.

18. Stitch the 47" piece of bias to the inside of the strap in the same manner.

19. Attach the 9" strip of hook and loop tape (or side by side strips, if you are using 1"-wide tape) midway down the front of the strap. This piece of tape is used to attach the utility pouch you create in the next project.

Try on the lunch tote for size. Figure out what should go in all your pockets. Do you have one of those fancy knife/fork/spoon-type pocket knives that you can stick in the front pocket? What are you bringing for lunch? This item might encourage a little more outdoor dining, which means less clean-up for everyone. So spread a blanket in the yard for supper tonight and pretend you're on a far-away exploration. You might find your mental list of to-dos shrinking and your presence with your kids growing.

Tool Roll and Nature Pouch

Tool Roll and Nature Pouch

This functional tool roll and zippered pouch can carry everything any explorer might need, such as notebook and pen, compass, pocket knife, magnifying glass, or maybe an emergency energy bar. With this pouch, you can examine, dissect, and discover nature to your heart's content.

We have already established the fact that we love hiking with our kids. For both of our families it really is some of the best times we share as a family. There is something about the space, the fresh air, and the endless possibilities for exploration that bring us all to our true best selves individually and as a family too. And the outdoors diffuses some of the noise just a little bit. (There's a reason we call them "outdoor voices"; indoors those same voices can make you cringe.) Outside it all feels just fine. And if it's not just fine, at least you can move a little bit further away.

Take this little nature pouch and utility roll on your next hike. We've added hook tape tabs to both so that you can attach them right to your lunch tote. (You can attach it easily to the lunch tote.) These handy accessories make exploration, inquiry, and discovery second nature for the entire family.

● **Finished Measurements:** 5½" × 3" zippered pouch and 8½" × 6½" tool roll ●

Supplies

¼ yard of medium-weight fabric such as denim or canvas

Note: Choose fabric that looks good on both sides. The bottom of an old pair of khakis or jeans is a great source of fabric.

¼ yard quilt-weight fabric for the contrasting lining in the utility roll

5" of hook and loop tape (the partner with the tape used in the lunch tote project)

Small elastic hair band for the utility roll

6" invisible zipper for the pouch

Part One

This nature tool roll really does encourage exploration and makes a kid feel like a young scientist. Kids really enjoy the idea of carrying a bunch of gadgets for the express purpose of digging around in nature and exploring and recording what they turn up. It makes the whole idea of a hike much more gratifying.

Discuss with your child the kinds of things he or she might require when out on a hike. Suggestions include a sketch pad and pencil for drawing and recording flora and fauna. Maybe your child would like a pocket knife for whittling or dissecting a discovered owl pellet. We know what kind of things we want on the hike. What do your kids want with them?

Steps

1. Cut two 9" × 7" pieces of the medium-weight material for the backing and the pocket.

2. Cut one 9" × 7" piece of the quilt-weight fabric for the inner lining.

3. On one of your medium-weight pieces, fold the long edge over 1½" toward the right side. Press and then make a second 1½" fold.

4. Press this fold and then edge stitch ⅛" from the first fold to secure. This is your pocket piece.

5. Decide how you would like to subdivide the pocket. Using a washable marker, mark lines at the desired positions.

6. Lay the lining piece out with the right side facing up. Place the pocket piece on top, right side facing up as well. Align the bottom and side edges.

7. Baste stitch the layers together, ⅛" from the aligned edges.

8. Stitch over the marked lines. Make sure to backstitch at the beginning and ends of the stitching. (See the illustration.)

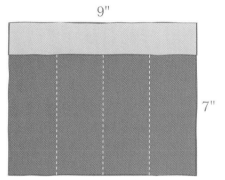

Measure and mark where you'd like your pocket lines to go, then stitch over your marked lines.

9. Cut 2½" of hook and loop tape. Set the loop tape aside. On the back of the second piece of medium-weight fabric, position the hook tape smack dab in the center of the rectangle. The long edges of the loop tape should be parallel to the short edges of the fabric.

10. Hand-stitch the elastic hair band to the center of the piece of hook tape. This completes your backing.

11. Place the backing and the lining/pocket pieces together, right sides facing.

12. Beginning in the middle of the bottom edges of the aligned rectangles, stitch all the way around the piece, ¼" from the edge. Leave a small opening for turning (about 2") at the end of your seam.

13. Trim the seam allowances around the corners. Turn the pouch right side out and tuck in the raw edges of the opening. Topstitch around all four sides, about ⅛" from the edges.

Now fill the pouch full of supplies, roll in either side of the pouch so that each rolled edge meets in the middle, and secure it closed by looping the elastic band once or twice around the middle of the rolled up pouch. Then attach it to your lunch tote using the hook and loop tape.

Part Two

The second part of this project gives you someplace to hold important things such as money or a phone or essentials that really need to be kept tight. A zippered pocket is good, too, for keeping special items found on the trail, such as an extraordinary rock or a colorful bird feather. Whether you are 7 or 47, having a special pouch with a hidden zipper always feels a little like having a special secret.

Steps

1. Cut a 6½" × 6½" square of the medium-weight material.

2. With the right side facing up, center a 2½" piece of hook and loop tape on the square. Stitch into place.

3. Attach the hidden zipper, using our handy dandy diagram. You should end up with a tube that is held together with the invisible zipper.

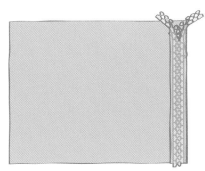

Sew zipper, face down, to right edge of the right side of your square, just to the right of zipper teeth.

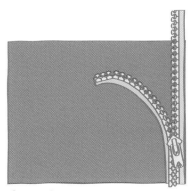

Open zipper.

Pull unstitched-down side of zipper over to left side of fabric, line up with edge, and sew just to the left of the teeth.

Flip right side out and zip up.

4. With the wrong side facing out, arrange the tube so that the zipper is centered relative to the long edges. Press. Open out the zipper just enough for turning.

5. Using a ¼" seam allowance, stitch the short edges together. Zigzag finish the edges to prevent fraying.

6. Clip the seam allowance around your corners.

7. Open the zipper and turn the pouch right side out. Press.

Attach this handy nature pouch to your lunch tote and fill it with your essentials.

Part Three

Now it's time to pack your lunch and hit the trail. Load up your tool roll with a pencil and mini-sketch pad. Dig out the magnifying glass. Sharpen the pocket knives. Even if your first foray with the pouch is only into your backyard, you should have everything you need for some good exploration followed by a little nosh in nature.

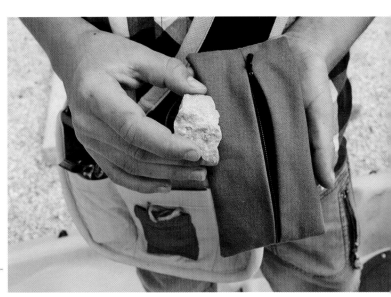

Upcycling Hat

Who doesn't like a hat? Really, even non-hat people kind of wish they were hat people, don't they? And for any family that's ever had a bad hair day, a hat—this hat in particular—is the perfect remedy.

Aside from the aesthetics, we live in Texas where going out in the summer sun without a hat is asking for trouble. The sun in your eyes and beating down on your head can really cut an outdoor excursion short. So not only will you look good as a group, but you can stay out all day if you want to. In a crowded setting you'll have no trouble distinguishing the little heads that belong to you from the masses out there in the fields, in the woods, or at the beach.

• **Finished Measurements:** Adjustable 20"–22" hat •

Supplies

¼ yard each of two different polyester knit fabrics with a one-way stretch. We recycled an athletic tee.

A scrap of heavy-weight interfacing or sturdy fabric such as vinyl or heavy denim to add structure to the brim. If purchasing, ask for a ⅛ yard cut.

Part One

Discuss your family colors. What works for you all as a group? Do you want to be matchy-matchy? Or do you prefer complementary colors? Do you want to put some kind of family logo or insignia on the front of your hats to let the entire world know you are a unit? Keep in mind, too, that for identification purposes having bright colors is a definite plus, especially when you're in a crowded setting such as a festival or on a beach.

Now hit up your dresser drawers, the local thrift store, or maybe a neighborhood garage sale in search of the right color fabrics for your family.

Part Two

We stick to cutting on this day so you don't need your sewing machine yet. Have fun with this process. Because the pattern pieces are so small, this is a good project for learning the art of using a pattern.

Steps

1. Trace the pattern pieces from page 144 onto a heavy paper such as a file folder or cereal box and cut them out.

2. Trace the brim pattern onto one of each color fabric you are using.

3. Trace the brim onto your heavy-weight structural material. (It won't be visible when the hat is complete, but it helps stabilize the brim.)

4. Trace the crown piece four times onto each color you are using. For example, if you are using blue and orange you need four blue pieces and four orange pieces. Make sure to cut the pieces in the direction of the stretch as indicated on the pattern.

5. If you are using any type of embellishment, such as the strip shown in the photo, cut it to the desired size. We used a 1" strip on the front pieces in our sample. If you are duplicating this style, cut a 2½" × 6½" strip. Fold the strip in half lengthwise, right sides facing in. Stitch ¼" from the long edges leaving the short end open. Turn the tube right side out and press.

Take a break now if you are pressed for time. Assess moods. Determine hunger. Check your own level of readiness. Ready? Move ahead. No? Pause and call it a day.

Part Three

This is a great kid project because it is has several of those magic moments where what you are making slowly appears before your eyes. It is a simple project, but the idea of making a hat, especially this one, feels really advanced.

Steps

1. Fold each of your crown pieces in half with the right sides together, and sew ¼" from the short curved edges. Start stitching at the top of the hat and sew down to the folded outer edge, backstitching at the bottom. (See the illustration.) Reopen the piece after sewing.

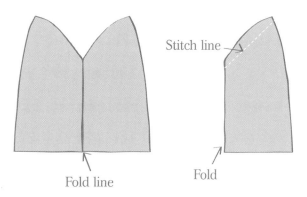

Stitch line

Fold line

Fold

2. If you are adding embellishment, measure 1" from the bottom of one stitched crown piece and attach the embellishment. To make the embellishment as shown in our sample, fold the long edges of the strip of fabric and press. Then pin the strip into place on the crown piece and edge stitch ⅛" from the top and the bottom edges of the strip. Don't worry about the raw edges as you'll catch those in another seam later.

3. Now place two contrasting pieces of your opened-up sewn crown pieces and place them with the right sides together. Stitch one edge from the top of the point down to the bottom with a ½" seam allowance. If you are making this hat for a little baby head, use a larger seam allowance. Sew a contrasting pair exactly like the first, with the same color on top and the stitching on the same edge.

4. Stitch the other two pairs, but this time with the opposite color on top (but the stitching on the same edge).

5. Take two of the paired pieces you've just created, place the good sides together and sew around the half circle using a ½" seam allowance. Make sure your colors are alternating. (Again, if you're making a hat for a smaller head, use a larger seam allowance.)

6. Repeat this with the other set of pair pieces. See the magic? You should now have two domes that will be about the right size or slightly too big for your head. Put them aside or try them on in their silliness. If you can actually keep your kids from trying them on, let us know because that is just about an impossible feat. Now onto your brim.

7. Place the knit brim pieces together, right sides facing. Place the heavy-weight structural material on top of the paired pieces. Stitch along the outer edge of the brim (the half circle) with a ½" seam allowance.

8. Trim the seam allowance to ⅛" (this cuts bulk and makes for a cleaner curved edge). Turn the brim right side out and press.

9. Stitch ¼" from the outside (convex) curved edge of the brim. If desired, you can sew an additional two or three rows of evenly spaced stitching to stabilize the brim and give it a sporty look.

10. Select one of the domes to be the outside of the hat. If you have added an embellishment, that might be your front. Align the bottom edge of the dome with the raw edge of the brim with the right sides together and pin. The brim should be centered relative to the piece that will be in the front. Make sure you have the color scheme going the way you want it. (See the illustration.)

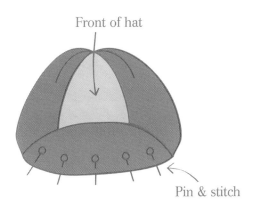

Front of hat

Pin & stitch

11. Stitch the layers together, ⅛" from the aligned edges, making sure to capture the entire edge of the brim.

12. Place the two dome pieces together with the right sides facing. Make sure to tuck the brim up into the hat. Line up the fronts and backs as you want them. Pin all the way around. (Kids often hate pinning, but it makes the process of sewing way easier and definitely more regulated.) Make sure you have the brim properly captured in the pinning.

13. Starting at the back of the hat, sew all the way around the bottom of the hat, leaving a 2" space in the back of the hat for turning.

14. Turn your hat right side out. Top stitch all the way around the base of the hat.

15. If the hat is a bit on the large size, create a tuck in the back of the hat and stitch.

Now you're ready for some serious cycling. Or upcycling. Or just hanging out and hiking (or lounging in the backyard) with the family. Can you just imagine the family portrait you'll get with all of you sporting your super matchy family caps?

chapter 6

fun and games

We know, just as every parent knows, that running and maintaining a family can be a lot of work. There are endless tasks, errands, chores, and issues to be dealt with. There are a lot of personalities to keep up with and a lot of responsibilities as well. All day and all week long, in family life there are so many needs that must be met that it's hard to remember the fun in it all.

We also know that family life is better, easier, livelier, and more connected when there are fun and games involved, and we're grateful for the random reminder. It doesn't matter whether we are playing with the kids or just setting them up for some fun, imaginative play of their own. There's no doubt that family life is better when we take time to play.

We are big believers in leaving kids to their own childhood play and imagination and not interjecting too much of ourselves into their creativity. We have seen some of the most amazing inventions and ideas come out of the times when our kids are totally immersed in kid world. There is something to a kid's imagination that is unique to childhood, and we appreciate that. Because we appreciate it so much, we also work hard at making sure we don't put our big parental thumbprint on our kids' play. Sure, we're here for them, but sometimes we like them to feel like we're not.

At other times, we realize that some of our most fun family connection can come from the times we are willing to get involved and really play and enjoy time with our kids—either one-on-one or with the family as a whole. When we're able to put all other tasks aside in the name of a little family fun and games, when we are truly willing and able to immerse ourselves in play, we are always glad we did.

We created the projects in this chapter for rainy afternoons. Or times when you need to get the wiggles out. Or lazy days. Or sick days. Or days when the kids' imaginative sides need a gentle nudge. We created these projects in order to inject a little more fun and games into family life—because sometimes we all need a little reminder about that.

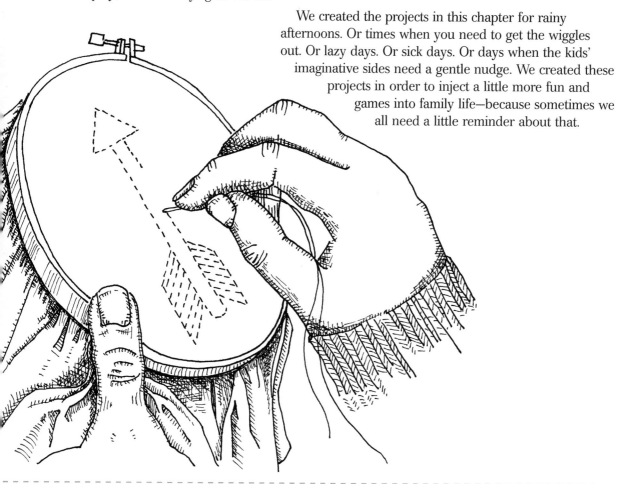

Game Board and Caddy

Game Board and Caddy

We love playing board games. No matter the season, it's a great way for our families to slow down and connect with each other. Whether as a group, or broken off into pairs, board games are a great way for us to relax, with a little friendly competition thrown in! Unless moods call for a more cooperative game, which is a mood that's hard to ignore.

This particular game caddy offers several serving suggestions, which is good because dispositions and ages can dictate just what game is on the table at any given moment. The caddy's portability has also proven handy and served us well on many a road trip and other family outings.

Part of the fun of the creation of this piece is that it can be a montage of favorite fabrics. Do you have a sentimental piece from a garment your child grew out of? Or a remnant from a baby blanket? Maybe Grandma's tablecloth is kicking around just waiting to be called into action. Whatever you use, in the spirit of the games, keep it fun.

• **Finished dimensions:** 28 ¼" × 15" •

Supplies

- 2⅜-yard cuts of quilt-weight cotton in contrasting colors (you can choose any combination you like, but for the purposes of these instructions, we refer to them as "red fabric" and "black fabric")
- ¼ yard of a quilt-weight cotton for the backgammon board divider and the ties
- ½ yard of fusible adhesive (also called webbing)
- ⅝ yard of heavy-weight cotton fabric such as denim or khaki
- 16" of hook and loop tape

Part One

The first part is all about the checkerboard. Because this project is made up of different game elements, we've tried to break the project down by element as much as possible. You can kind of zen out (or zone out as the case may be) on today's process of cutting strips of fabric and sewing the strips back together, too.

Steps

1. Cut four 2¾" × 25" strips from the red fabric.

2. Cut four 2¾" × 25" strips from the black fabric.

3. Place a red strip and a black strip together, right sides facing. Align all of the edges. Stitch together, ¼" from one of the long edges. Repeat for the other three red/black pairs.

4. Open the pairs. Press the seam allowance against the darker side (in this case, black).

5. Place two of the pairs together, right sides facing, with the red edge of one aligned with the black edge of the other. Stitch and press as described in Steps 3 and 4. Repeat for the other two pairs. The result is two four-strip rectangles.

6. Place the two four-strip rectangles together, right sides facing, with the red edge of one aligned with the black edge of the other. Stitch and press as described in Steps 3 and 4. The result is one eight-strip rectangle.

7. Cutting across the alternating strips, cut the rectangle into eight 3" strips. (Don't cut along the stitch lines; cut across the stitch lines.)

8. Place a pair of strips together, right sides facing, so that red pieces are facing black pieces, and the seam allowances are pointed in opposite directions. Stitch together, ¼" from one of the long edges.

9. Press the seam allowances open. Align, stitch, and press a third strip as described in the previous step. Keep adding strips, one by one, until all eight pieced strips come together to make a checkerboard. It should be about 18½" × 20", but don't worry if it is off by a half inch or so.

That's it for Part One. Now go get your game on. Or make dinner. Or whatever brings about the greater good for the family.

Part Two

In this part we work on the backgammon board. Kathie has never played backgammon at all, but Bernadette has spent many ruthless hours playing bouts of backgammon with her brothers—especially in the summer months. (Don't ask her about the gambling summer in which she lost lots of paper route money to a childhood visitor from the big city.) If you've never played before, it's a really fun and quick game. And it's just right for filling those little chunks of family down time without committing your whole afternoon to one activity.

Steps

1. Use the pieced checkerboard as a pattern for cutting out the backgammon board. Lay the checkerboard on the heavy-weight fabric, right sides facing. Pin together. Cut the heavy-weight fabric around the edges of the checkerboard. Remove the pins and separate the pieces.

2. Place the fusible adhesive on top of the triangle cutting pattern on page 145 with the paper side facing up. Trace all of the lines of the pattern and then shift the paper over and trace again so that you have 12 triangles side by side. Repeat to make a second 12-triangle set. (See the illustration).

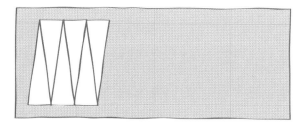

First tracing

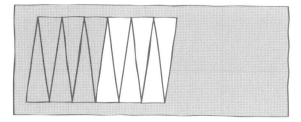

Second tracing

3. Cut out the parallelograms along the outer edges. Place one on the wrong side of the red fabric and fuse according to the manufacturer's instructions. Repeat with the other set for the black fabric. Cut the triangles out along the lines.

4. Cut an 18½" × 1½" strip from the strip/tie fabric.

5. Fold under ¼" of each long side of this strip and press.

6. Fold the backgammon board piece so that the shorter edges are aligned. Press to make a crease in the center. Place the strip over the crease and stitch along each long side of the strip to sew it in place. Trim away any fabric overhang.

7. Lay out the first set of triangles as shown in the illustration and fuse into place.

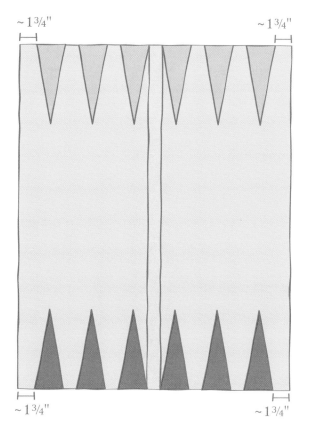

8. After the first set of triangles is ironed on, stitch around the edges of the triangles using a small- to medium-width zigzag stitch. (You might want to practice on scraps before stitching so that you can optimize the stitch settings to get just the look you want.)

9. Lay out the second set of triangles as shown in the illustration. Fuse and zigzag-stitch as described for the first set.

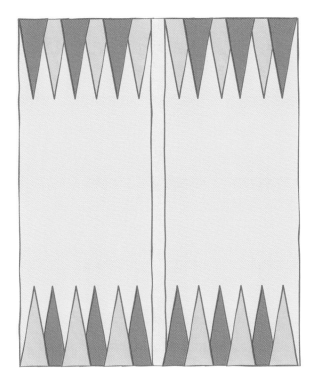

Part Three

In this part we make the pocket for the game pieces, what we like to call the piece pouch. Clever, right? In this pocket you can keep chess pieces, checkers, playing cards, a score pad, and pencil. Hook and loop tape keeps everything tidy and neat. Imagine such a thing! A game set with all its pieces in one place. It's positively dreamy.

Steps

1. Cut two 14" × 17½" pieces of the heavy-weight fabric

2. For each piece, fold one of the shorter edges over to the wrong side ½" and press, and then make a second ½" fold and press again. Stitch into place about ¼" from the first fold. (We did a double line of stitching but that's just decorative. You can do that or not do it.)

3. Lay out one of the pieces so that the wrong side is facing up and the folded, stitched edge is on the left side. Fold the top long edge over 1" to the wrong side and press. Make a second 1" fold and press again. Stitch into place, about ¼" from the first fold. Repeat Step 3 for the second piece of fabric, but this time start out with the folded, stitched edge on the right side. After this step, you should have mirror image pieces.

4. Cut four 4" pieces of hook and loop tape. We are going to make a series of folds to use as gauges for positioning the hook and loop tape and to use as stitching guides later. Fold both pieces in half lengthwise so that the long raw edge is in line with the long folded edge. Press to make a sharp crease.

5. On one piece, center a piece of hook tape on the thick fold between the crease and the outer edge of the thin fold. Stitch into place. Center a second piece of hook tape on the thick fold between the crease and the raw edge. Stitch into place. (See the illustration.)

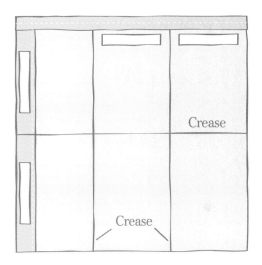

6. Repeat Step 5 on the other piece of fabric, this time using loop tape.

7. The next step is to fold the pieces into thirds widthwise. For each piece, make a fold 5" from the outer edge of the thick hem. Press. Bring the short raw edge over to meet this fold and press.

8. On the piece of fabric with the hook tape, center a piece of hook tape just below the thin fold between the crease and the raw edge. Stitch into place. Center a second piece of hook tape just below the thin fold between the two creases. Stitch into place. (Refer to the illustration after Step 5.)

9. Repeat Step 8 on the other piece of fabric, this time using loop tape.

10. Check your creases on at least one piece. If they are still visible, you are good to go. If not, you should re-press and possibly even mark the lines with a washable marker.

11. Put together the right sides of the two denim pieces and stitch ¼" from the short, raw edges. Zigzag-stitch the raw edge to prevent fraying.

12. Flip the pieces right side out. Work the seam between your fingers to fully roll it out. Press, taking care to avoid the creases. Align all of the edges, and put the corresponding hook and loop pieces together.

13. Sew across the long lengthwise crease from the thick hemmed edge to the edge with the seam. Make sure to backstitch at the beginning and end of the stitching. (See the illustration.)

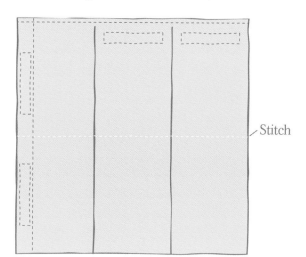

Stitch

14. Stitch along the widthwise creases from the thin hemmed edge to the first line of stitching.

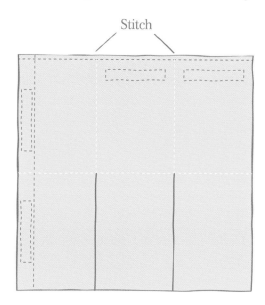

Stitch

15. Stitch the layers together from the thick hemmed edge to the widthwise stitching, a little over ½" from the thin hemmed edge.

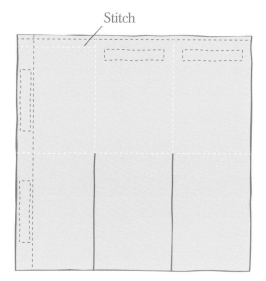

Stitch

16. Cut the tie/divider fabric into four 2" × 20" strips. Fold the strips in half widthwise, right sides facing in. Stitch ¼" from the long edge and one of the short edges (or, if you prefer a frayed look as shown in the photo, leave both short edges unstitched). Trim the corners (if applicable) and turn the tubes right side out. Press. If you wish, you can tie the ends into knots as shown in the photo.

17. On one side of the pocket, position the end of one tie along the raw edge of the pocket 2" from a corner. Leave about ¼" overhang and stitch into place, ⅛" from the edge. Repeat with a second tie 2" from the other corner. Flip the pocket over to the other side and repeat with the remaining ties, making sure the ends are in line with the first set of ties. Pin the ties to the pocket so they do not get caught in the stitching in the next step.

18. Now you're going to make a fabric sandwich. Place your backgammon board face up on your work surface. Arrange it so the long edges are at the top and bottom, and the shorter edges are on the sides. Place the pocket piece on top of the backgammon board so that one edge of the

piece pocket meets up with the left side of the backgammon board. Make sure the edges line up. Place the checkerboard face down on top of the piece pocket making sure that all the edges of the checkerboard line up with the backgammon board. Pin all the edges together to keep them lined up while stitching.

19. Starting in the middle of the right edge of the backgammon board (the edge without the piece pocket) sew all the way around, ¼" from the edges, leaving a 3" opening for turning. Make sure that you catch the piece pocket in the seam when you get to the other side.

20. Trim the seam allowances at the corners and then flip the board right side out.

21. Tuck in the raw edge of the opening and press. Top stitch all the way around, ⅛" from the edges.

That's it! You did it. You can roll your game caddy up and tuck it away for a rainy day or break it out now and get in a little family game time. Or give it to the kids to play around with so you can get dinner on the table.

Bean Bag Toss

Bean Bag Toss

Have you mastered the fine art of juggling yet? Or maybe you've decided that you'd like to start with something just a little bit simpler? Either way, this bean bag toss game is for you. All you need is a doorway and a few juggling balls and you will get a whole afternoon (or morning or evening) of fun. If you haven't yet done our juggling balls project, no worries; even crumpled-up newspaper works for this game. Whether you have big children or little (or big children who appear little or little children who happen to be big—you get the idea), this point-tallying bean bag toss just might raise the spirits in your household. Just don't stand on the wrong side of the doorframe!

Part of the fun of this game is its carnival-esque feel that is reminiscent of a long-ago era of backyard carnivals and fun fairs. Bernadette grew up with a group of older girls in New Jersey who could get the entire neighborhood involved in their weeks-long, charity-driven, little backyard carnivals. If they had seen this bean bag toss, their hearts would have leaped at how easy fundraising would have been with this little gem.

● **Finished Measurements:** 31" × 28" ●

Supplies

1 yard of burlap for the banner front

1 yard of cotton ticking (or any other medium- to heavy-weight woven fabric) for the banner back

⅛ yard of light- to medium-weight fabric for the hanging strip

1 yard of light- to medium-weight fabric for the rings

¼ yard light- to medium-weight fabric for the point circles

Number stencils, fabric markers, or a fabric that stands out against the point circle fabric

1 yard iron-on adhesive (also known as fusible webbing)

1 package of ½"-wide double-fold bias tape

32" dowel or other stick approximately ½" in diameter

Part One

This project is pretty simple with just a few "huh?" moments here and there. You can choose any pattern of fabric you want, of course, but we recommend finding something with a bright carnival feel. Before you begin cutting and sewing, take a look at the photo and get a feel for how everything is laid out. It is, as with many of our projects, up for some personal and artistic interpretation.

Steps

1. Cut a 30" × 28" piece of burlap.

2. Cut a 30" × 28" piece from the backing fabric.

3. Place the backing fabric on top of the burlap with the wrong sides facing and stitch around the perimeter about ½" from the edge.

4. Cut a 29" × 4½" piece of medium-weight hanging strip fabric.

5. Fold both of the short edges of the strip cut in Step 4 over ½" to the wrong side and stitch into place, ¼" from the folds.

6. Fold one of the long edges over ½" to the wrong side. Press.

7. Align the raw edge of the strip with the top edge of the banner. The right side of the strip should be facing the burlap side of the banner. Stitch together, ½" from the aligned edges.

8. Working on the back side of the banner, align the folded edge of the strip with the line of stitching you just made. Pin into place. Flip the banner over to the front side and stitch through all layers, ¼" from the seam. Take care to make sure the stitching catches the strip on the back side.

Now is a good time to take a break because you have a recognizable banner-type thing that could actually be hung as is. A feeling of completion is always nice.

Part Two

Circular breathing is a big part of a good meditation process. Circular cutting is a big part of bean bag toss making. This part is all about the circles—cutting them out and then cutting them out once again. We've given you dimensions, but feel free to play around with the sizes a bit. This is also a good time to play around with a compass—especially if you have a couple of kids around to play with. You could also round up a variety of different sized dishes, bowls, and cups and simply trace around them. There is something so intrinsically cool about a perfect circle.

Steps

1. Draw a 14" diameter circle on the paper side of the fusible adhesive. Draw a 9" circle in the center of this circle.

2. Draw a 12" diameter circle just beside the first circle. Draw an 8" circle in the center of this circle.

3. Draw an 8" diameter circle just beside the second circle. Draw a 5" circle in the center of this circle.

4. Cut along the lines so you have three "donuts" of fusible adhesive. Place them on the wrong side of the fabric you're using for the rings and fuse according to the manufacturer's instructions. Cut the fabric around the inner and outer edges.

5. Remove the paper backing and position the circles on the burlap. You can use the same configuration shown in the photo or position them as you like. Fuse the circles into place and stitch around the outer perimeters using a small zigzag stitch.

6. Using a straight stitch, sew around the inner edge of the circle, about ⅛" from the edge. This stitching prevents slipping during bias tape attachment.

7. Cut the burlap and backing layers at the edges of the inner circles.

Whew. Did you hold your breath a little? We did. Cutting right through the center of a project holds a bit of scariness. Take a deep breath and exhale, circularly if you can.

Part Three

This is the home stretch and then it's game time, people. So start warming up your arm a little and get ready for some family competition. Um, we mean fun.

Steps

1. Cut a 36" piece of 2" bias tape.

2. Apply bias tape to the circles as described in the appendix.

3. Draw three 5" circles onto the paper side of the fusible webbing.

4. Fuse the adhesive to the point circle fabric according to the manufacturer's instructions. Cut out the circles around the lines.

5. Stencil or draw the numbers 5, 10, and 15 directly onto the fused circles. Alternatively, you can draw the mirror image numbers onto the paper side of the adhesive, fuse to the contrasting fabric, cut out and fuse to the circles as shown in the photo.

6. Position the circles on the project. As usual, you can follow our placement or you can come up with your own.

7. Using a narrow zigzag stitch, sew around the perimeter of each circle.

You did it! We know that bias stuff is tricky to describe and read, but after you get going it makes sense. Right? If Bernadette can do it, anyone can.

Now hang your masterpiece in a doorway somewhere and start playing! If there are little ones around they might even volunteer to be your catcher.

Art Roll Up

Art Roll Up

Of all the things in our house that we have made over the years, this one is perhaps our most utilized. Every time we need mobile art supplies, whether we're going on a road trip, on a plane ride, to a friend's house, or just to spend a little time in the yard, this art roll is definitely ready to go. It's small, but it's proficient and completely portable, too. You can fill it with whatever drawing materials suit you best—pencils, markers, crayons, pens, or a combination of all of these things. The larger pockets on each side provide space for a sharpener, an eraser, and a bottle of glue so that your little artist can create a collage with all the leaves, wrappers, brochures, and maps that come your way.

Creating artwork on the road is different than doing art projects in the home. Because supplies are more limited than they are at home, the artist has to call upon a certain level of creativity. And sometimes, depending on the players and the moods, of course, the art sessions can actually go a little deeper because the focus is on the creating and not the materials.

This art roll project makes a great gift for birthdays or for siblings of a new baby. For a household with a new baby, this roll up can provide a little bit of order and provides nice impetus for some art activity for the overwhelmed sibling. It's a great gift for all ages, too—from very little people all the way to grandmas. We highly recommend making a few and stocking them away because everyone needs an emergency gift every now and again. Except us, of course. We always plan ahead and allow ample time to make gifts and have scheduled activities for all our children. Ask anyone. Except on those days we don't plan ahead and then you'll find us whipping up a gift the morning of the party.

● **Finished Measurements:** 14½" × 21½" ●

Supplies

½ yard of light- to medium-weight fabric for the roll-up exterior piece and interior pocket pieces

Note: We used the polyester knit from an old thrift store garment, but this pattern would work just as well with regular cotton, canvas, or old sheets.

½ yard of light- to medium-weight fabric for the roll-up interior piece and tie pieces

1 to 6 15" pieces of rickrack or ribbon (optional)

Part One

This is a simple project, and it's good, too, for practicing long, straight lines. You can easily help a novice sewer or hold a wee one on your lap while you run it through the machine.

Steps

1. Cut a 15" × 22" rectangle from each of the two fabrics.

2. Cut two 7½" × 15" rectangles from the exterior/pocket fabric. For each rectangle, fold one of the long edges over ¼" to the wrong side. Make a second fold 1" from the first fold.

3. Stitch each fold into place, about ⅛" from the first folded edge. These two pieces are pencil pockets.

4. Place these pieces atop the 15" × 22" piece cut from the interior fabric. The wrong side of the pocket fabric should be facing the right side of the interior fabric. Orient these pocket pieces so that they are at opposite ends of the interior fabric, 15" edges in line, and pin.

5. Measure 2½" from the short edge of one of your pocket pieces and draw a straight line from the top of the pocket to the bottom (make sure to use a washable marker).

6. Measure 1" from that line and mark another line.

7. Repeat Step 6 10 more times so that you create markings for 12 little pencil pockets. Stitch through the pocket and interior layers, right over the lines.

8. Now do the same thing on the other pocket.

Part Two

As soon as the pencil pockets are sewn the kids will want to stuff the pockets full. Maybe they've already done so. Who can blame them? Look how cute those pockets are and how they beckon for writing implements. You need to take the pencils out, though, to finish the project. Make sure to get any little tiny pencil nub that has wedged itself down in the bottom corner.

Steps

1. On the back of the second 15" × 22" piece (the one without the pockets) attach your rickrack in whatever design you want. Feel free to copy ours or come up with your own configuration. You can also embellish with appliqués or letters or whatever else you can dream up.

2. Fold the two 1½" × 14" pieces in half lengthwise with the right sides together and press.

3. Sew each piece along one short end and all the way down one long side, ¼" from the edges.

4. Turn the pieces right side out and topstitch all the way down the open long side.

5. Place the two ties side by side on top of the interior piece with the short raw ends in line with the 22" edge of the interior piece. The tie pieces should be approximately 5½" from the end of the large piece of fabric (about 1" below the top of the pocket). Pin the ties in place and stitch, about ⅛" from the aligned edges.

6. Place the interior and exterior pieces together with the right sides facing and pin. Make sure the ties are tucked inside.

7. Starting in the middle of one end (any end will do), sew all the way around the edge with a ¼" seam allowance, stopping just about 2" from where you started.

8. Trim the seam allowances around the corners. Turn the pieces right side out and press.

9. Tuck in the raw edges at the opening and topstitch all the way around, about ⅛" from the edge.

10. Fold the roll in half, end to end, and roll it up so it's fit to be tied.

That's it. You're finished. Now give each other a high five and call it a day.

Part Three

Break out your vessel of drawing supplies and dig through. (Come on, you know you have a giant and unruly box of crayons, pens, and pencils all mixed together. They're just begging for a little order.) Have everyone choose a few of their favorites and fill the pockets with each person's selections. Find a pencil sharpener or head out to the art store and treat yourselves to a super nice metal sharpener like the real artists use. While you're at the store, maybe you can get everyone a sketch pad of their own, too. Or you can make one from the paper you have at home.

Head on out to the yard or the front porch and have a little family sketch-athon. Mix it up by handing the drawings around in a circle in a game of collaborative drawing. It's one of our favorite things to do.

Juggling Balls in a
Drawstring Sack

Juggling Balls in a Drawstring Sack

When we are stuck inside on a super hot or rainy day, there are all sorts of things we can turn to as a family. Board games often come out for a duo or for the whole family. Cards also play a role. And we do lots and lots of drawing, too. But sometimes we need to move our bodies, so we need an indoor activity that is physical.

Learning to juggle can make for a very goofy afternoon of super family fun. And if the parents are learning at the same time the children are, the laughs are pretty uproarious. There is nothing a kid likes more than watching their parents put themselves in the kind of silly, compromising positions of learning a new skill. These juggling balls, which double as hacky sacks, are really perfect for those stuck-inside kinds of days.

These balls are simple to make and can be made with any small scraps of material of any colors. They also make a great birthday gift for friends.

● **Finished Measurements:** Three balls 3½" in diameter and one 5" × 10" bag. ●

Supplies

For the bag:

⅜ yard of fabric (or 2 pieces of scrap fabric larger than 6" × 11") for your drawstring bag

1 piece of string, binding tape, ribbon, or an old shoelace approximately 24" long

1 safety pin to pull the tie through the channels

For the balls:

6 small scraps of quilt-weight fabric at least 9" × 4" (these can be all different or all the same color, your choice). If purchasing fabric off the bolt, ask for ⅛ yard of each fabric.

2½ to 3 cups of dried beans or rice

Kitchen funnel

Note: *You can also just roll up a piece of paper like a funnel if you don't have an actual funnel.*

Part One

For simplicity's sake, we start with the drawstring bag. This is just a basic drawstring bag so it is a good project for even the most beginning of sewers. There are lots of straight lines and easy hems, and there's plenty of fun to be had by threading the string in the bag (that's an especially great task to work those little fingers). This project provides immediate gratification, too, so it can help spur a real love of sewing.

Steps

1. Cut two 6" × 11" pieces of the bag fabric and put them together with the right sides facing.

2. Starting approximately 1½" from the top of one 11" side, stitch around three sides of the pouch. Your line of stitching should stop approximately 1½" from the top of the second 11" side.

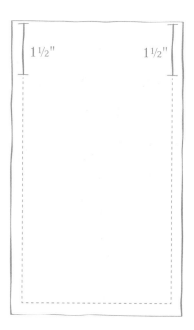

3. Place the pouch on the ironing board. On one long edge of the pouch, separate the layers of the seam allowance, and press the top layer against the top of the pouch. Maintain the ½" fold at the unstitched top portion (see the illustration). Repeat on the other long edge and then flip the pouch over and press the edges on the other side.

Press seam allowance open ←

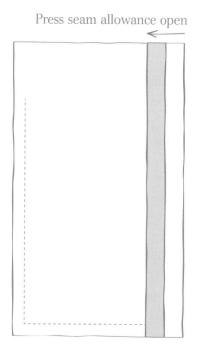

4. Fold the top edges of the pouch over ½" to the wrong side, press, and then fold another ½" and press again.

5. Stitch about ⅛" from the first folded edge, making sure to leave room for the string to be threaded through this channel.

6. Clip the bottom corners and turn the bag right side out.

7. Use the safety pin to thread your tie through the channel, tie the ends together, and voilà! You have a drawstring bag.

These bags are handy, so you might consider making a few of them for other small toys that need to be collected into sets.

Part Two

This is a good family project as some of the steps, such as filling the bag with beans, can be done by even the very wee ones in the house. Some steps, though, take a little bit of manipulation, so adult hands are definitely required.

Steps

1. Trace the pattern from page 146 on a piece of paper and then cut out the pattern.

2. Trace the pattern onto your fabric (or fabrics—this is your Fabric A, which can either be the same fabric for each piece, or six different pieces, or anywhere in between!) six times and then cut out the pieces. Make sure to cut out the notches shown on the pattern.

3. Place two of the pieces together in a perpendicular fashion with the right sides facing. Make sure to align the notches. (See the illustration.)

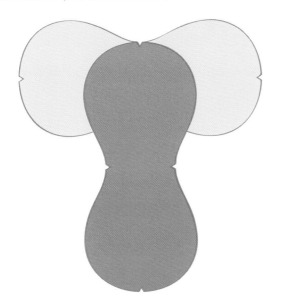

4. Carefully and slowly stitch all the way around the edges using a $\frac{1}{4}$" seam allowance, leaving 1" open for turning and stuffing. As you sew you should be continuously manipulating the fabric so that the next set of notches match up and the curved edges stay aligned.

5. Turn the ball right side out.

6. Using a kitchen (or paper) funnel, fill the bag with the beans or the rice.

7. Turn in the edges of the opening and sew it closed using a whip stitch.

8. Repeat Steps 3 through 7 until you have three completed balls.

Part Three

Now it's time to get playing. If you know how to juggle, share that skill with your kids. If you don't, there are some great places online to find information about getting started.

These balls are also great for any variety of bean bag toss games and for hacky sack. Line up a few various sized buckets or other containers and mark them with different values. Boxes from recently purchased beverage 12-packs can serve as a great device for bean-bag targets. (Now you know what to do with at least ONE of those boxes.)

chapter 7

happy birthday to you!

We love birthdays. We love the chance to reminisce on the actual day of birth and look ahead at what's to come. We love the fact that everyone gets one day—their very own day—just to celebrate being born. And we love stretching that one day out into the days before and after in order to make sure the celebration and the honoring is truly felt and understood.

As parents, we have had enough experience with kid birthdays and birthday parties to understand what is important to us. Neither one of us really goes for the big crazy crowds of kids hopped up on sugar. Nor are we comfortable going to the places created for the purpose of hosting a kid party. We like to keep it home if we can. And we like to keep it kind of simple, too. Adding a little bit of structure, some games, or a project helps us in our quest for maintaining some semblance of order—without dominating, of course! We're not saying we don't like festivity and celebration, but we both know that chaos just doesn't work for *us*.

Although we are not wont to do big parties, we do want our kids to really feel the celebration. We want them to think of their birthdays as a time for wishing a little bit and for dreaming about the future. What do I want? Where will I go? What do I want to do? Who will I see this year? We love birthdays, too, as a time for looking back and thinking about how far we've come and where we've been. It's fun for kids and adults alike to take a minute to pause in reflection about what they've learned, done, seen, heard, and created in just one year's time.

We have seen our kids get a little wonky in their behavior as their birthdays approach. One minute they're happy as can be; another they're feeling a little dismayed at the aging process. We've seen a seven-year-old proclaiming she's done aging and wants to just stay seven for a while. We've known a twelve-year-old who wished time would speed up and she could be fourteen next. And then there's the forty-four-year-old, well, never mind . . . By giving kids a chance to really mark the transition of birthdays, we think we help make the process a little easier. Sure, kids are excited to move on, but they're also sometimes a little hesitant to leave the past behind. Just like their parents.

We created the projects in this chapter to give us a way to really mark this time in life when the old is fading into past and the future is standing there wide open and ready to be received. We created these projects to weave a common thread through our families' birthday celebrations and to create family tradition on this day of celebrating each family member's individuality. Finally, we created these projects because we love birthdays!!!

Reversible Birthday Crown

Reversible Birthday Crown

Ah, the birthday crown. We love this project so much. We love it not only because it's super easy and fun to make but also because of what it does for the feeling of tradition we like to create in our family celebrations. In both of our households we kind of revel in having continuity in our birthday celebrations from year to year and from kid to kid. Our kids also love knowing what's coming, knowing what they can look forward to, and knowing that they are a link in this family chain. If they don't like it, then they do a good job pretending because they all know how much their respective mothers really love and need our birthday traditions. They're such good little children.

The fact that this crown is reversible means that it can work for one and all family members. You can make one side girly and the other more masculine. Make one side quiet and the other one loud. Make one side dark and the other light. Whatever elements you have on one side, you can create the opposite on the other, thereby covering all your bases. Which side is exposed changes from family member to family member and even from year to year.

Now that we think about it, maybe this pattern could be like a mood crown! It could then be used not just for birthdays but for everyday use as well. Each person could have his or her own mood crown and, at a glance, everyone in the house could see from afar just what kind of mood the wearer is in.

● **Finished Measurements:** 20" unstretched
(crown accommodates head sizes toddler through adult) ●

☆ Supplies

⅜ yard (or a scrap that is at least 16" × 12") light- to medium-weight fabric for one side of the crown

⅜ yard (or a scrap that is at least 16" × 12") light- to medium-weight fabric for the other side of the crown

⅜ yard (or a scrap that is at least 16" × 12") heavy-weight material, such as denim, home décor fabric, or even heavy-weight interfacing to add structure to the crown; this piece does not show on the outside of the crown, so don't worry too much about appearance)

⅛ yard (or a scrap that is at least 7½" × 2½") of light- to medium-weight fabric for the scrunched strap

A few buttons that coordinate with the fabric you choose or the type of mood you want to create with the crown

16" of rickrack or other embellishment for each side of the crown (optional)

3¼" of ¾"-wide elastic

Paper for tracing pattern

Large safety pin

Embroidery floss

Part One

This project can be as detailed or as simple as you like. It's totally your call. Discuss with your kids what you want to do. Have a little family drawing session. If you are working with more than one child, have each kid spend time drawing out ideas for the two sides of the crown. Or, if you're feeling particularly family-friendly and compatible, you can all work together to come up with the designs.

Steps

1. Select your buttons and your other embellishments such as rickrack, ribbon, and whatever else you can dig up.

2. Select your fabrics. Remember you need two different fabrics to set two different tones or moods.

Note: *This is for birthday parties, so choose some fun fabrics. Vintage curtains can be fun to cut up for this project. Maybe you have a nice piece of old upholstery or some 1970s bed sheet that you've tucked away somewhere. Maybe even an old skirt of yours that you've had tucked away in the drawer since you graduated from college. Come on; you know you're never going to wear that thing! Why not make it into a birthday crown?*

3. Trace the pattern piece on page 146 onto paper and cut it out. Fold one of your exterior fabric pieces in half widthwise. Place the pattern on the fold as indicated, pin, and cut. Repeat for your other exterior fabric and your heavy-weight structural material.

4. Cut a 7½" × 2½" strip from the strap fabric.

5. Cut your rickrack, ribbon, and other design pieces. We used a star inside a circle. See how festive it looks? You can replicate this or come up with your own design.

6. Play around with your embellishments and decide which buttons and other pieces will go on which side of the crown.

Part Two

This is a fun part of the project because in it you begin the embellishment process. Have fun playing around with it. Maybe let your kids do one side and you do the other, or let each person select and add a piece for each side.

1. Pin your rickrack, ribbon, and any other design pieces to the right side of the crown pieces and then sew them into place. (You add the buttons later.)

2. Pin your structural material piece to the wrong side of one of the exterior pieces. Baste stitch the pieces together.

3. Fold the strip of strap fabric in half lengthwise with the right sides facing and stitch ¼" from the long edge.

4. Turn the tube you just created right side out. Press.

5. Cut the elastic to a length of 3¼". Insert the safety pin into the end of the elastic and then guide it into the tube. Pull the elastic through until just a bit of elastic is showing at one end. Stitch into place about ¼" from the end of the tube.

6. Bring the elastic the rest of the way through and remove the pin. Arrange the elastic so that just a bit is showing at the end of the tube. Stitch into place as described in the previous step.

7. Lay the joined fabric/structural material crown piece out with the right (exterior) side facing up. Place one end of the scrunched band ½" beyond the short straight edges of the crown/structural material. The bottom of the band should be about ½" above the bottom edge of the crown (see the illustration). Stitch the band into place, ⅛" from the crown edge.

8. Place the second exterior piece on top of the first exterior piece (and the attached band) with right sides facing. Starting on the bottom edge of the crown near the short edge without the elastic, stitch along the entire perimeter with a ¼" seam allowance. Stop about 2" from where you began. If it helps, you can mark that spot before you begin sewing so that you know where to stop. This opening is for turning and elastic insertion.

9. Trim the seam allowance down to about ⅛" at the crown points, taking care to not cut the stitching. Snip the seam allowance at the three "valleys" between the points. Also trim around the corners on the short side edges.

10. Flip your crown right side out, making sure that the denim is sandwiched between the two fabric pieces. If needed, use the end of a pin to pick out the crown points. Work the edges between your fingers to fully roll out the seams. Arrange the allowance at the opening so it is flush with the rest of the edges. Press.

11. Insert the raw end of the scrunched strap into the opening so that it is about ½" beyond the folded edges. Pin into place.

12. Starting at the position of the elastic, topstitch all the way around the perimeter of the crown, ⅛" from the edges.

Steps

1. If you are using buttons, now is the time to put them in place. If you are putting buttons on both sides of the crown, hold the two buttons together on either side of the crown, back to back.

2. Using embroidery floss, sew them into place using a simple knot, sewing through both sides if applicable (see instructions on page 139).

3. Now you can send out the invites to the party!

4. Okay. Now you're finished. (See what we mean about being able to finish this in Part Two?)

Part Three

We could have put this part into Part Two, and we know you know that. But we really feel that after Step 12 on Part Two you might need a little rest. Or some protein. Or any kind of sustenance, even if it's a breath of fresh air. We encourage you to pause and fill your proverbial cup.

The party begins when the celebrant dons this crown, whether there are guests invited or not! Or, if you've made the crown and you just can't wait for a party, perhaps your family could declare a random king or queen of the day.

Anticipation Calendar

Anticipation Calendar

The Anticipation Calendar has definitely become a regular and welcome part of our birthday rituals. The calendar gives us a visual countdown to the birthday so the kids can see exactly how many days they have left. It also lets us stretch the celebration out to more than just one day so we can truly commemorate an entire birthday week. Although receiving presents is fun, the Anticipation Calendar takes a little bit of the focus off the "what do you want?" question and puts in more on the idea of "who am I?" The birthday becomes less about the gifts themselves and more about the honoring of what has been and what we hope will be. It sounds pretty lofty, but you'll see it's quite simple really.

Here's how it works. The calendar counts down the week prior to the birthday. There are seven numbers and on each number there are two strips of paper or cardboard. There are two pockets; one is called past and one is called future. Or lessons learned and wishes. Or whatever phrases you want to use that best capture the feeling for your birthday celebrant.

On each day in the week before the birthday, the celebrant looks at the year past and asks him- or herself, "What have I learned? What did I do? Where did I go? What did I accomplish?" The celebrant writes that idea on the little card and puts it in the past pocket. After observing this tradition for a couple of years we have realized that taking some time for reflection is perfect at birthdays. It's way nicer than just tweaking the list of expected gifts. Not that there's anything wrong with gifts; we love them! But having all the focus on acquisition can sometimes feel a little tedious and empty, too.

After the question about the past is answered, the celebrant then asks, "What do I hope to learn? Do? See? Accomplish in the coming year?" These questions give the birthday boy or girl (or man or woman) a chance to dream a little bit and imagine just what this next year might hold, to write it down, and to put it in the future pocket.

On the celebrant's actual birthday we read the past and future cards. We then write them down in the Family Records book, which is one of the projects in Chapter 8. If you have a life journal for your kids or a baby book, you could write them in there, too. Several years of lists become a great chronicle of each person's growth. When the kids are little the lessons learned are so tangible: walking, talking, riding a bike, and so on. As the kids age the lessons can be a little more subtle and encompass big emotional changes as well as physical feats.

• **Finished Measurements:** 17" × 26" •

Supplies

½ yard burlap (or a piece that is at least 17" × 26") for the calendar base

½ yard (or a piece that is at least 14" × 22"—a fat quarter would work great) quilt-weight fabric in a happy print and celebratory colors for the calendar background

⅜ yard of quilt-weight fabric for the circles

¼ yard of quilt-weight fabric for the star pockets

⅛ yard (or 3 scraps that are at least 2" × 6") of heavy-weight fabric such as vinyl upholstery or denim

⅛ yard of quilt-weight fabric for the stamped stars and pocket welts

Fine tipped, washable marker

Pinking shears

14 small safety pins

14 small rectangles of cardboard

Fabric number stamps or a fabric pen

Iron-on adhesive (also known as fusible webbing)

Hole punch

1 stick or dowel to hang the finished banner

Note: *In most cases, you can use bed sheets or old shirts or whatever small scraps you can find instead of using the pieces of the quilt-weight fabric. Only the 14" × 22" piece needs to be whole. All the others can be comprised of smaller scraps. Using an old garment or baby blanket of your children's is a good way to bring a little sentimentality into the project.*

Part One

This is a project that can be as detailed as you like or as simple as you need. The colors you pick should be celebratory and worthy of hanging in your home for a week at a time. We went sort of carnival-esque with ours by using an old striped bed sheet and a men's shirt. Because you will be using this banner year after year, it might be a good idea to stay away from patterns your kids might outgrow.

Please note that any of the stars and circles can be replaced by any shape you choose. Make it yours or copy ours as you see fit (patterns for the stars are provided on page 147).

Steps

1. Cut a 17" × 26" rectangle from the burlap.
2. Cut four 1" × 3½" strips from the ⅛ yard cut of fabric.

Note: *Make these next cuts with pinking shears.*

3. Cut a 14" × 22" rectangle from the quilt-weight fabric for the background.
4. Cut two 9" circles from the ⅜ yard cut of fabric. Use a compass to draw the circle, or simply trace a dish or a bowl with a 9" diameter.
5. Use the pattern on page 147 to trace two 7" stars on the ½ yard cut of fabric and cut them out.
6. Trace seven of the 3" stars from page 147 side-by-side on the paper side of the iron-on adhesive. Cut out the stars.
7. While you have your pinking shears out, it is a good time to go ahead and cut the three 2" × 6" heavy-weight strips as well.
8. Fold the four 1" × 3½" fabric strips in half lengthwise, right sides together. On one side of each strip, make marks ¼" from each short end. (See the illustration.)

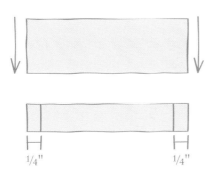

9. For each large star: With the right side of the star facing up, center one of the strips with the folded edge just about touching the upper "arm" edges (see the illustration).

Folded edge

10. Stitch from one mark to the other, exactly ¼" from the folded edge (be sure to backstitch). Align a second folded strip with the first folded strip, raw edges touching. Again, stitch from one mark to the other, exactly ¼" from the folded edge (see the illustration).

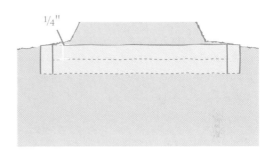

¼"

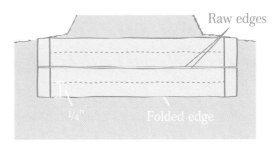

Raw edges

¼" Folded edge

11. Flip the star over to the wrong side. Center a 2"-long line right between the two rows of stitching. It should start ½" after the beginning of the stitching, and end ½" before the end of the stitching. Connect the endpoints of this line with the endpoints of the stitching lines (see the illustration).

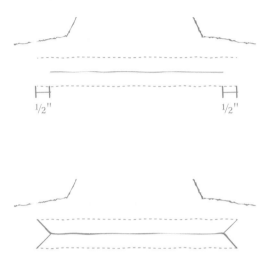

12. Carefully cut along the lines on the wrong side of the fabric. (Tip: Fold the star in half to get the snip started and then work your way out.) Press the edges back as shown in the illustration.

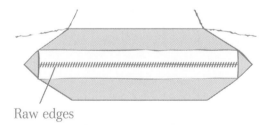

Raw edges

13. Bring the raw edges of the strips over to the wrong side and press.

14. Flip the star over to the right side and topstitch very close to the edges.

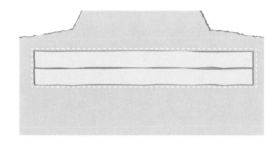

15. Pile all your pieces together and roll them up in the burlap because your work is done for now.

Go take a walk. Get the mail. Play a game. Drink some water. Have a snack.

Part Two

This part requires less measuring and more just looking at the design and laying out the pieces until you have what you want. Because it's so freeform there is no exact way to compose the banner; just eyeball it. This part of the process helps develop the kids' design sensibility. Let them lay out the pieces as they like.

Steps

1. Position each large star in the middle of the 9" circles and stitch all the way around about ¼" from the pinked edges. Stitch through both layers to form a pocket as shown in the photograph. Don't worry too much about the shape; just make sure it is large enough to accommodate your cardboard pieces.

the middle. The short ends of the pieces should overlap the banner front by about 1". Fold the pieces in half from the front side of the banner to the back to form the tabs for hanging the banner.

7. Sew the vinyl pieces into place with a rectangle of stitches. Be sure to capture both sides of the tabs.

That's it for now. Take a nap. Read a story to your children. Or just sit outside and stare up at the sky together.

Part Three

As you can see, you're practically finished. If you're like us, you might be making this calendar the day before the birthday week begins. Or maybe even the day of. No worries, you're almost there. And if you're not near a birthday, this part can either wait until a birthday approaches or you can do it now in preparation.

Steps

1. Put one pin on each numbered star.

2. Cut 14 pieces of cardboard. Ours are 2" × 1½".

3. Punch a hole in the tops of each piece of cardboard with a hole punch.

4. Stick a safety pin through two pieces of cardboard and pin one set to each star.

5. Now you are ready to let the birthday week begin!

Have fun counting down, reflecting, and dreaming about the future.

Note: You can also use this calendar for countdowns to other big events. Put it to work any time your family needs to reflect or dream big! And if you want to count down but don't have time to make the big calendar, no worries. Get some markers and pins and a piece of cloth and make a simple substitute until you can get to the big project. The effect is the same. If you think it can't be simple, you should see the one Bernadette made for her family! It was composed from a small piece of canvas from an old army cot with two small squares for pockets and seven little diamonds cut from vinyl. What it looks like isn't as crucial as what the project brings to your family celebrations.

2. Position your circles at the top and bottom of the 14" × 22" background rectangle (as shown in the photo, or however you like) and stitch all the way around.

3. Using the fabric stamps, stamp numbers 1 through 7 on your small stars. (Check out page 139 for information on stamping fabric.) Alternatively, you can use fabric pens to write the numbers on the stars. You can also label your large stars as "past" and "future" as shown in the photo.

4. Peel the backing off of the numbered stars. Position them on the background rectangle in either numerical or random order. Be wonky or linear as it suits you. Fuse into place.

5. Center your decorated fabric background on the burlap rectangle and stitch all the way around, about ¼" from the pinked edges.

6. Position and pin your three vinyl rectangles along the top of the burlap. Place two of the pieces 3" from each corner and put the third piece in

Pin the Tail on the Donkey

Pin the Tail on the Donkey

There is a vague memory—okay, it's actually rather vivid—of a 10th birthday party where the game of "pin the nose on the smiley face" was played. It was the 70s, after all, and the smiley face in its big yellow splendor was all the rage. Somehow I was embarrassed about the game, even though now it seems kind of cool. I had wanted pin the tail on the donkey. What I got instead was a game made up by my mom with the poster from my bedroom wall and a sock for a blindfold. It probably wouldn't have mattered what she did actually; I was 10, and in my mind it was the dawning of the age of embarrassment.

This version of Pin the Tail on the Donkey will definitely be a repeat customer at your children's birthday parties and will not cause one smidgen of embarrassment. And if your friends don't make their own game, they will definitely want to borrow yours. Because of its cool look, it might even hold a permanent place on a bedroom wall—that is if you take down that smiley face poster.

Pin the Tail on the Donkey is such a classic game it can be considered retro. This project might even inspire you to hold a completely retro-themed party. You could play Pin the Tail on the Donkey and musical chairs, eat cupcakes, and call it a day. You might even find yourself mixing fruit juice and ginger ale in a glass bowl. Just don't forget to put on a pretty apron before you do.

Because of the tactile aspect of this particular version of this game, it's important that you have some rules, which means blindfold those kiddos and spin 'em around a little and let 'em loose in the direction of the board. Make sure you only let them use one hand, though. Otherwise that second hand is feeling all around and sensing the edge and the shape of the donkey and, well, before you know it, there's a pile of tails in exactly the right spot. And that just kind of takes the fun out of it. When you use only one hand wherever it first touches is the spot for the tail. So make sure one hand has the tail and the other one is held behind the back.

Now get out there, team, and WIN!! We mean, um, have fun. And happy birthday!

● **Finished Measurements:** 20" × 23" ●

Supplies

1 yard (or a piece that is at least 24" × 21") of medium- to heavy-weight fabric for the backing

½ yard (or a piece that is at least 14 ½" × 21") of light- to medium-weight fabric for the main front fabric

⅜ yard (or a piece that is at least 10" × 21") of light- to medium-weight fabric for the top and bottom borders

2 42" lengths of rickrack in different colors and widths (optional)

½ yard (or a piece that is at least 14" × 18") of light- to medium-weight fabric for the donkey and the tail strips (a fun print is good here)

½ yard iron-on adhesive (also known as fusible webbing)

6 pieces of felt in different colors that coordinate with your fabrics

A dowel rod or other stick for hanging the donkey on the wall

String or twine for hanging

6 small safety pins

Part One

This project has lots of little pieces to cut and some fun zigzag work. We start with the tails, which might be putting the cart before the horse (or donkey, as the case may be), but it wouldn't be the first time we've done that.

Steps

1. Cut a 28" × 2" strip from the "donkey" fabric.

2. Fold in half lengthwise, right sides facing in, then stitch ¼" from the aligned long edges.

3. Turn the tube right side out

4. Arrange the tube so that the seam is on one edge and press.

5. Cut the tube into six 4½" pieces and set them aside.

6. Using the patterns on page 148, cut one of each of the following from the six different colors of felt: 2" diameter circle, 1½" diameter circle, and 2" leaf shape.

7. On each of the 4½" sewn strips, position a 1½" felt circle at the top and a matching teardrop at the bottom as shown in the illustration. Pin the felt pieces into place.

8. Starting at the bottom of the leaf shape, run a small tight zigzag stitch right down the middle of the strip to the center of the circle. Backstitch several times at this position for added stability and then continue stitching up to the top of the circle.

9. Cut the border fabric into a 6" × 21" strip and a 4" × 21" strip for the bottom and top borders. On the 6" × 21" strip, measure 1½" from the bottom of the fabric and, starting 1½" from one side, position and pin one of your 2" felt circles. Repeat on the other side. Position and pin the other four circles in a line between the first two, leaving about 1" between each circle. Using a tight zigzag, stitch all the way around the perimeter of each circle.

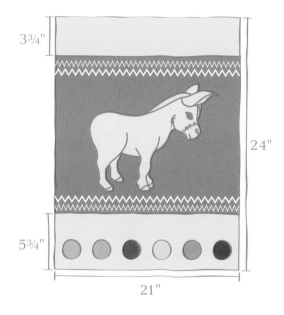

Part Two

In this part we make the donkey, which is pretty fun to do. When was the last time you traced and drew out a barnyard animal? Never? Well, now's your chance.

Steps

1. The donkey pattern is provided on page 148. Isn't he so dang cute? Kathie drew him. Free hand. That's just how she rolls. Trace the donkey onto the paper side of the iron-on adhesive. You can just trace the silhouette, or can include the interior detail lines as well. Fuse the adhesive to the

wrong side of the donkey fabric according to the manufacturer's instructions. If you are planning to stitch the details, hold the donkey up to a window and use a washable marker to mark the lines on the right side of the fabric. You could also use a permanent marker and simply draw the lines on the fabric.

2. Cut a 14½" × 21" rectangle from the main front fabric. Peel away the paper backing and position your donkey in the middle of the rectangle. Fuse into place.

3. Using a tight, small zigzag stitch, sew all the way around the perimeter of the donkey adding detailed stitching as shown if desired. This is totally optional, and the donkey looks cute with or without it. You make the call.

4. Measure ½" from the bottom edge of the main fabric and attach one piece of rickrack across the bottom edge. Repeat on the top edge.

5. Measure 1" from the bottom edge of the main fabric and attach another piece of rickrack. Repeat on the top edge.

6. Place the strip with the sewn circles face down on top of the main fabric. Align the top edge (long edge furthest from the circles) of the strip with the bottom edge (long edge below the donkey's hooves) of the main fabric. Stitch together ¼" from the aligned edges.

7. Flip down the strip and press.

8. With the right sides facing, align one long edge of the 4" × 21" strip with the top edge of the main fabric.

9. Stitch together and press as described for the bottom strip.

Part Three

In the case of this project, being in the home stretch means it's almost time for the party. If you're like us then you just might be doing this the night before your child's actual birthday. No worries. There's only a little bit left to do. Then you can ice those cupcakes and call it a night.

Steps

1. Place the pieced front and back rectangles together with the right sides facing. If needed, you can trim one piece or the other so they align perfectly.

2. Stitch the layers together ½" from the top edge, being sure to backstitch at the beginning and end of the stitching. Starting at the position of the top seam (where the top border meets the main fabric), start stitching down and around ½" from the edges. Stop stitching when you reach the top seam on the other side (see the illustration).

3. Trim the seam allowances around the bottom corners and then turn the piece right side out through one of the openings.

4. Tuck under and arrange the flaps at the opening so that they are in line with the side edges. Press.

5. Starting at one corner, stitch ⅛" from the top edge. When you reach the other corner, pivot and stitch down 1". Pivot again, and stitch across the banner to the other edge. Stitch back up 1" to the stitching start point. Also topstitch the edges from the bottom of one opening to the bottom of the other, ⅛" from the edge (see the illustration).

6. Pin your tails into place using small safety pins.

7. Insert the dowel in the top opening and tie the string to both ends.

Now fix your hair, put on your lipstick, and go answer the door. I think your guests are here!

Birthday T-shirt Party

We are no strangers to the kid birthday party of pretty much any variety. We have held the giant soirée with all the bells and whistles. We have held the just-one-kid-over-for-a-sleepover. We have had the family-only party. And we've had just about every type of party in between. We have no thoughts about which is best. Actually, we do, but we're really trying not to be judgmental.

Whatever kind of party we do throw or attend, we know that we are fans of parties of the homemade and homespun variety. This is partially because we're not really fans of commercial ventures (sometimes much to our children's dismay). It's also partially because we like to make stuff and make stuff up—the games and the cakes and the presents, too. And finally, if there's one thing we've learned over the years, it's that more is less. And in this case the less is the fact that just this one activity can really make up the entire party.

This party is definitely not for wee little kids, but even kids as young as five can have fun arranging precut pieces and helping to select fabrics and colors.

● **Finished Measurements:** Approximately 6 child-size t-shirts ●

Supplies

1½ (approximate) yards of fusible iron-on adhesive

Variety of fabric scraps at least 6" big

Note: It's easier to use fewer big pieces than more little pieces. Also, the more diverse the prints on the fabrics, the better.

Stencils, at least 2" tall, in a variety of letters and shapes

Pinking shears (optional)

1 t-shirt for each child in attendance—solids, stripes, whatever you like (you could even ask them all to bring their own if that seems easier)

Part One

The tasks on this day should be done before the party. It's a good way to begin the celebration without all the craziness of the party. If you have a bin of scraps, dig through and let your child pick out favorites. You can also use garments that are no longer in use. For sentimental purposes, using old garments of the child's can be a fun way to go. A patterned bed sheet is also good, especially when you can find some cool vintage print at the thrift store.

Steps

1. Select your fabric pieces with your child.

2. Cut the pieces into workable rectangles that are at least 6" big.

3. Iron the pieces of scrap fabric onto the fusible adhesive by following the manufacturer's directions.

Part Two

Depending on the age of the children attending the party this next step can either be done pre-party by the adults in the house or with the kids attending the party. Even if you have bigger kids do this step, it's a good idea to have a few ready-mades done ahead of time to serve as samples or extras.

Steps

1. Using stencils, or freeform drawing if you're up to it, trace a bunch of letters and shapes onto the fabric. If you're drawing freehand, make things such as stars, circles, and even random things such as zigzags or spirals. Letters for spelling out each child's name is a good start.

2. Cut out the shapes using a combination of pinking shears for the larger shapes and straight scissors for the more intricate shapes such as the letters.

If you happen to have access to a die-cut machine, the kind used at elementary schools and public libraries, you can use it to create some great shapes. We know not everyone has one, but it sure is fun if you can find one.

Part Three

It's party time! So pour yourself a beer. Oh, wait a minute; sorry, wrong party. Although, depending on the time of day you still might want a beer. We leave that decision up to you. After that, gather all the kids around a large table or other large flat space.

Steps

1. Have all the kids select their letters and shapes. To make it into a party game, put all the pieces into the middle of the table and let them take turns picking. Or plan an alternative version of musical chairs wherein the pieces are laid out randomly on the chairs and when the music stops, whatever piece is on the chair in front of you is the piece received. Add a new piece each go round, or come up with some other variation on the party game scene. What we know is that when it's party time, everything should be a party game. *Everything.*

2. After the kids have selected their pieces, it's a good idea to have some system of order so that their pieces don't get lost or confused with someone else's. It works well to give each child an envelope to hold his or her pieces.

3. Have each child lay his or her shirt flat in front on the table.

4. Let the kids arrange their letters and shapes in whatever arrangement they like. Encourage them to play a little with mixing it up a bit and being off-center. Not everything has to be the standard, right-down-the-middle kind of design.

5. After they have the designs they like, have the kids peel the backing off each piece. Help them pin the pieces in place.

6. Iron on the pieces. You can let young kids do this with supervision if you feel up to the task. If it makes you nervous, you can do it and let them watch. Truly though, this is a good task for kids to conquer as it makes them feel pretty powerful to handle such a dangerous tool.

7. This last step is optional but greatly adds to the longevity and to the cool look of the shirts. Run the shirts through the sewing machine going willy-nilly, back and forth, helter-skelter across the design. There's no need to go around each shape, although you could have at it if you really, really want to. We promise not to judge you.

It's time now for singing and presents and maybe a little fashion show, too. The cool thing about this party activity is that it's an activity and parting gift all in one, meaning that there is no need to go out and buy a bunch of j-u-n-k to put in a bag for each child that will end up in the trash in a week anyway. Good job. Now go get yourself some cake.

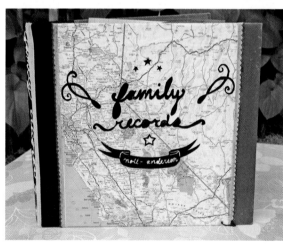

chapter 8

commemorate and celebrate

In an effort to make family life as fluid and fun as possible, we like to add celebration and commemoration where we can. We like to take moments for recognizing and rejoicing in the fact that we are indeed a family. We try to inject celebration into the commonplace because it makes it easier to get through each day. One of us (we won't tell which one) is even known for doing an occasional family cheer to raise spirits and boost morale. We can tell when family life needs a little boost by the level of whining or fighting that is happening. If we were mathematicians we might have some kind of morale equation figured out with which we would factor in the whining, multiply it by the number of people, add the numbers of hours slept or how much sugar was consumed, and divide it by how much celebrating of family life we've done. But we're not mathematicians, so instead we judge morale on a feeling.

Some of our commemoration is solemn and serious, but it's only as solemn and serious as a three- or five- or seven-year-old allows us to get. So really, our commemoration isn't very solemn at all (it's a best laid plans kind of thing). The reality of how we commemorate things has ended up being way more entertaining than the ideal would have been; it's more sentimental and personal than we ever could have imagined. And it's funny, too. So even when we think we should be all serious or somber, we bite our lips or laugh out loud and continue on.

We have realized that all our commemorative practices, banners, rituals, and icons serve to slow us down a little bit. They remind everyone in the family that we are all in this together; we're all on the same team. And because we're all here together, we might as well find ways to really enjoy the connection we create.

As mothers we have realized that our days with our small children are really quite fleeting. Half of our collective kids are about halfway or so to college age and/or moving out on their own. When they were two and three years old we kind of thought they'd be with us always and they'd always be exactly as they were in that very moment of time. Then, before we knew it, they were four and five and ten and thirteen and, well . . . you get the idea. Believe us, the fleetingness of time and all that stuff people tell you about when your baby is born is really true.

So, while we still have our little families in our little nests, we want to try to mark our connection where and when we can. We want to celebrate our association. We want to appreciate and acknowledge each individual while simultaneously recognizing and honoring the family as an entity. From that idea the projects in this chapter were born. By making these projects now and commemorating our families as they exist today, our goal is to continue our feeling of family connection long after our kiddos have flown the nest, for our own sake and for theirs. *Sob.*

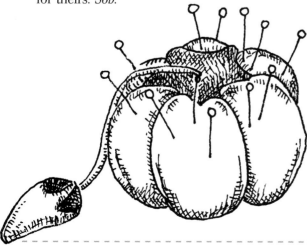

slow down.
connect.
enjoy! ✦✦
✦ ✦

Family Flags

Family Flags

You can make family flags for special family occasions, deaths, anniversaries of various types, big events, or just to give your family a chance to celebrate being a family. Making a family flag gives us all a chance to recognize what we love about family life and to put down in words or images why we are glad to exist as an entity. (Don't we all need a chance to ponder the whole existence thing on occasion?)

These flags have morphed significantly from our original design, but the idea and the intent is the same: to celebrate and honor being. The first flags we made were for a friend's birthday. A group of us were trying to think of a way to really pay tribute to her big day. The flags were simple, really; they were cut with pinking shears and barely sewn at all. Our friend loved the flags, though, and she still has them hanging right above her desk where they wave good wishes in her direction.

We have made a lot more flags since we made that first set. Our favorites are the flags we've made for our own families. Some of them have been of the quick-and-easy variety and others have been more highly stylized. Whether you go decidedly detailed or super simple doesn't matter. It's the message of warm wishes, sweet sentiments, and good feelings that counts.

There's an interchangeable component in the design of these flags that enables you to change the message of the flags and create them anew each time they are used. Because you can swap out the message, you can make one set of flags that you can use for any occasion or event.

● **Finished Measurements:** Six 8" × 6" flags ●

Supplies

½ yard quilt-weight fabric or 1 bed sheet for the flag backing and tabs

¼ yard each (or scraps at least 9" × 7" in size) of 6 different quilt-weight fabrics for the flag fronts

¼ yard of light-weight fabric that is white or light-colored for the message component

Pinking shears

Fabric markers

12 random or matching buttons

6' to 8' string or twine

Part One

This is a simple project but it has a few different phases of completion. Part Three is ongoing. For example, you might do it several times a year.

Before you begin your work, decide how many flags you want to make. Do you want to make one for each member of the family so that each person can write out his or her own message? Or do you want to make one for each day of the week? Talk about it together and decide. Our Supplies list includes enough material to make six flags, so if you intend to make more than that, you should adjust your quantities appropriately.

Steps

1. Using the pattern piece on page 149, cut out one piece of the backing fabric for each flag you're making.

2. Use the same pattern piece to cut one piece from each of the flag front fabrics.

3. Cut 12 4½" × 2½" rectangles from the same fabric you used for the backing.

4. Now take a break before you move into Part Two.

Part Two

This next part involves pretty straightforward sewing, and most of what you need to do is perfect for little sewers who have learned how to do basic stitching. Crafting with your kids can be challenging, so remember that the point of this particular project is to celebrate family. Hang in there if things are feeling frustrating or if the little people aren't cooperating as you like. Just try to appreciate the connection you're making with your kids. They'll be grown soon. And you'll look back on this time and sigh at how quickly it passed. Really, you will.

Steps

1. To make your tabs, fold each of the small 4½" × 2½" rectangles of backing fabric in half lengthwise with the right sides together.

2. For each piece, stitch along the open long side with a ¼" seam allowance and then turn each tube right side out. Press.

3. Top stitch ⅛" from the edge of both of the long edges. Fold the pieces in half so that the short raw edges are aligned. Press.

4. Lay the flag front pieces out with the right sides facing upward. For each flag, position the tabs 1" from the side edges with the short edges in line with the top edge of the flag (see the illustration). Pin or baste stitch the tabs into place.

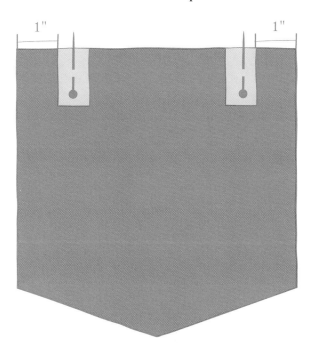

5. With the right sides facing, place the backing fabric over the front fabric and align all of the edges.

6. Starting in the middle of one of the longer sides of the flag, sew all the way around each piece with a ½" seam allowance, stopping 1½"– 2" from where you began stitching to leave an opening for turning the piece right side out.

7. Clip the corners.

8. Turn the piece right side out using the opening in the side. Tuck in the edges at the opening. Press.

9. Fold in the raw edges of the opening and edge stitch all the way around the piece, ⅛" from the edges. Make sure to catch the edges of the opening in your seam.

Take a break. Have a snack. Check your Facebook page. No, not really, don't do that. There's nothing on there you need to know right now. Well, alright, maybe have just a peek.

Part Three

This third part is really just one physical step. Everything else is mental work as you ponder which parts of family life you want to represent with your flags. What parts of your life do you want to celebrate? What wishes do you want to be picked up by the breezes? What are the things you appreciate about family? What things/feelings/places make your family feel like your family?

Steps

1. On each of the flags, sew two buttons approximately 1" from the top of the flag. Leave about 3½" between the two buttons.

Note: *You can sew the buttons the usual way, or use our cute tying method described on page 139.*

2. Using pinking shears, cut out six 4" × 5" pieces of the white or light-colored message fabric.

3. Near the top of each piece of message fabric, cut two slits for the buttons. The slits should run parallel to the side edges and be big enough for your buttons to go through. The slits should be about ½" from each side. For best results, hold the message piece over the buttons, and mark the desired position with a washable marker.

4. Using the theme that you and your family picked for your flags, write your wishes, sentiments, memories, or other appreciations on the message pieces.

Note: *If you're having a hard time thinking of ideas to use for your flags, here are some suggestions from flags we've created: things you appreciate about the celebrant; pictures of things the celebrant likes to do; haikus about family; single words that fit the celebrant; any words, drawings, or symbols that fit the mood or occasion.*

5. Attach the message pieces to the buttons, string up your flags, and let them fly!

This is a great project that you will appreciate time and again. Have fun with it. Hang the flags over your front door or over your kitchen window. Enjoy watching your family flags blow in the breeze and enjoy celebrating family life all year long!

Appreciation Banner

Appreciation Banner

One thing we have realized in the raising of our respective families is that life feels better when we appreciate more. We have also realized that sometimes the idea of appreciating is just a decision we make to change our perspective. We have figured out that when we live in a state of appreciation, it raises our energy level and shifts our focus to the positive. No doubt about it. How have we figured it out you might ask? Because we also have lived (and still occasionally do live) in a state of not appreciating.

When we are not appreciating, instead of feeling happy about what's working, we spiral into a state of focusing on what's not working. Things such as what chores aren't getting done, who's whining, or who isn't doing what we need them to do become our focus. The same holds true for everyone in the family. The more we focus on what isn't working or going our way, the more those things become our focus. When we find ourselves in this state we can use it as a reminder to appreciate one another and to break out the family appreciation banner.

The idea for this banner was definitely born out of necessity. We weren't sitting around pondering how we could amp up the existing joy for our families. Instead we were desperate and really, really needed to come up with something to shift the energy. What we've found with this tool is that when we appreciate more we often find there is more to appreciate. Why? Two reasons: 1. Because kids and partners almost always rise to our level of expectation. 2. Perspective really is everything. So when we expect good and appreciate more, we then get and see more good and more appreciation. Really. It's the truth, from our perspective.

Let us know after you've made this and implemented it in your home if you feel a shift for your family. And don't forget to appreciate your amazing self as well!

● **Finished Measurements:** 26" × 22" ●

Supplies

1 large burlap bag, or ¾ yard burlap

1 fat quarter quilt-weight cotton fabric

1 4" × 5" piece of scrap fabric for each family member, plus a few extras; if purchasing fabric, ⅛ yard yields several pockets

Note: *Pockets cut from old jeans work great.*

Pinking shears

¼ yard iron-on adhesive (also known as fusible web)

¼ yard light-colored fabric

Fine-tipped permanent marker for making labels

Note: *You can use stamps and fabric paint as an alternative to the labels.*

3 large buttons, random or matching

Embroidery floss and needle to attach buttons

⅛ yard (or a 6" × 6" scrap) of heavy-weight cloth such as denim or canvas

1 30" stick

Note: *Any stick will do. You can even use a stick you find outside as long as it's relatively straight and sturdy.*

Part One

If you don't have any burlap on hand then this segment might be all about taking a little field trip for material acquisition. Look in your phone book and locate any coffee roasters in your area. In our fair city it's kind of hard to throw a rock without hitting a coffee roaster—big or small. Sometimes even cafes are roasting their own beans and so burlap bags are in great abundance. Call various locations and ask if they have any extra bags available. It has been our experience that the coffee roasters are usually more than happy to be rid of the bags—especially for a family craft project!

Part Two

First you need to discuss how many pockets you need. Then, in this part, you only need to cut and iron; there's no sewing involved. Cutting and ironing are good tasks for kids. Sometimes cutting fabric can be difficult for little fingers, so help them by holding the fabric tight and showing them how to angle their scissors properly.

Steps

1. Cut a 22" × 26" rectangle of burlap. To help you cut it straight, pull out a few strands of the burlap at the measured spot. By pulling it out you create a line on which to make your cut. This is a very satisfying process.

2. Fray the edges of the burlap by pulling out a few more strands.

3. Using pinking shears, cut an 18" × 22" rectangle of the quilt-weight fabric.

4. Using pinking shears, cut as many pockets as you need from the scrap fabric. You should have at least one pocket for each family member. (Include your pets, too, if you like.) You also need one pocket for holding supplies. You might also have one for the world and one for the community. (These topic headings are up to your determination. Add the things and people that are

important to you and your family.) Cut the fabric to be either pocket-shaped (triangulated on the bottom) or just rectangular. They can be varied in size and shape, too, if you want. Let each family member pick out a fabric that he or she feels represents them. Or have the kids pick out fabrics for everyone. It's always kind of interesting to ask the kids what patterns they feel represent the different family members.

5. Using pinking shears, cut three 2" × 6" strips of the heavy-weight cloth. These are the tabs for hanging the banner on the stick.

6. For pockets marked with stamps, refer to the stamping instructions on page 139. For pockets marked with tags, fuse the iron-on adhesive to the light-colored cloth according to the manufacturer's directions.

7. Using pinking shears, cut one 1½" × 4" rectangle of the light-colored, adhesive-fused cloth for each of the pockets you cut in Step 4.

8. On each rectangle, use the fine-tipped permanent marker to write the name of a family member, pet, community, or other designated group or individual. Make sure to label one pocket for supplies.

9. Iron the name tags onto the appropriate pockets.

Part Three

As you're doing this project, bring up the subject of appreciation. What does it mean? How does it feel when we're appreciated? How does it feel when we appreciate someone or something else? You could even do a round of appreciations at the craft table: Have everyone go around and say one thing they're appreciating about themselves and about the process, too.

Steps

1. Place the 18" × 22" piece of quilt-weight fabric on your work surface and position your pockets as you would like them. Play around with locations and patterns. Pin the pockets in place.

2. Stitch around the sides and the bottom of each pocket. Be sure to backstitch at the top on each side.

3. Center the quilt-weight fabric rectangle on the 22" × 26" piece of burlap, pin it in place using plenty of pins, and sew around the perimeter of the fabric.

4. Fold your 2" × 6" hanging tabs in half so the short ends meet and the wrong sides are together. Put a pin in the middle of each tab so they stay folded. Center one of your tabs along the top edge of the burlap and hand-stitch it into place using one of the buttons and embroidery floss (see button tying instructions on page 139). Measure 6" to the right from the middle tab and attach a second tab in the same way. Measure 6" to the left from the middle tab and attach the third tab.

5. Run the stick through the tabs, and you're ready to hang your banner.

There you go! You did it. Fill the supplies pocket with a couple of pens and some small strips of paper. Make the paper long enough so that the strips stick out of the top of the pocket to serve as a visual reminder that there's some appreciating going on.

We fill out random appreciations for everyone and put them in the pockets. You can either have a specific time for this or you can just let it happen organically. Usually when one person starts writing notes of appreciation there is a snowball effect and the appreciations just start flowing. At week's end, perhaps during breakfast or dinner on one weekend day, hand each person his or her stack of appreciations and take turns reading them aloud. I said it before but I'll say it again, be sure to appreciate yourself as well.

We would love to know how this banner works for you and your family. We love ours. Sometimes we put it away and we forget about its existence. Then we take it out again when things are low and we get right back on the appreciation band wagon again.

Family Talisman

Family Talisman

Talisman: n. 1. An object held to act as a charm to avert evil and bring good fortune. 2. Something producing apparently magical or miraculous effects (definitions courtesy of Dictionary.com).

Usually when we think of a talisman we think of a small amulet or good luck charm. The two definitions we've given are why we chose the word talisman. We want this project to bring your family good fortune and produce magical effects. Maybe it'll even provide an occasional miracle.

When we return home after being out in the world all day, it's sometimes hard to remember to enter the family thoughtfully, slowly, and kindly. Perhaps we're tired from a long day. Maybe we're feeling rushed to make dinner for our hungry family. Maybe we're just shedding our public faces as we cross the threshold—letting our hair down so to speak, which isn't always pretty. Some days it takes a little magic and some serious intention to smoothly make the transition.

To prevent the family-as-whipping-post syndrome, use this family talisman as a reminder that home can be the well from which we draw inspiration, motivation, and satisfaction; it's not the drain. Use it to help you remember that family connections make us stronger, more clever, more creative, and definitely more beautiful, too. So, if you want to honor your family AND be more beautiful, you should totally make one of these.

Simple elements are layered to give a look that is complex, yet harmonious (just like a family). The main components of the talisman are 3 b's—base, background, and branches. The background shape is sewn atop the base, and the branches are sewn over the background shape. Surrounding the branches are clear pockets for photos and items specific to each member of the family. The banner can be further personalized with name labels, embroidery, and appliqués.

Hang your creation on the front door to serve as a reminder to you and each member of the family that you are home and that being home is a good thing. Use it to serve as a reminder to be nice to each other and to appreciate each other and to let visitors share in that understanding. Use it to celebrate all the individual pieces that make your family whole.

It might be just the miracle you're seeking.

Note: As with the Family Records book, this project is definitely open to creative interpretation. We want you to make it about your family, to speak of you. We've given you instructions for the one shown here, of course, but we want you to interpret the directions according to your family's needs. Let the talisman hold your family's wonders and let it serve as a window to all. Let it tell all who come to your door, "Here we are."

● **Finished Measurements: 32½" × 30"** ●

Supplies

¼ yard of clear vinyl

Note: A plastic blanket storage bag of any size, such as the bag that a blanket is packaged in when you first purchase it, is perfect for this project.

¾ yard quilt-weight fabric (you could use a bed sheet or tablecloth) for the front base piece

¾ yard quilt-weight fabric (you could use a man's dress shirt) for the background piece

¼ yard light- to medium-weight fabric for the branches

⅛ yard white or light-colored quilt-weight fabric for the small name banners (if you are making more than 6 labels, you need ¼ yard)

¼ yard white or light-colored quilt-weight fabric for the large name banner

1 yard medium- to heavy-weight fabric (such as denim, canvas, or home décor fabric) for the backing and hanging loops

¼ yard iron-on adhesive (also known as fusible web)

1 package of extra-wide double-fold bias tape (½") or ½ yard of quilt-weight or home décor fabric for making your own ½" bias tape (see instructions on page 139)

Embroidery floss of any color

Fabric letter stamps and/or fabric markers for labeling and adding detail

Tracing paper (for stitching on vinyl)

Stick or dowel for hanging the finished project

Part One

This part is about getting your design in mind. You can sketch it out on the inside of a brown paper bag or on another large piece of paper. You might want to call a family meeting to generate ideas. Or, you might just want to do it on your own when everyone else is in bed. Do whatever feeds your craft desires and keeps the family happy unless, of course, those two statements are oxymorons. In that case, well, you'll have to figure that out on your own.

Start by figuring out who's in your family. Will you add pets? The universe? Next decide what type of branches will connect you. Kathie used a strong solid tree—it represents her family's grounding and their love of nature. You could add branches for each family member, or simply group members around the branches as you see fit.

You also need to decide what shape you would like your background to be. We used a crest shape that looks like an open book. You can replicate this or look online or at the library for images of family crests and other inspiring designs. You can even use a simple rectangle or diamond.

Now play around a little bit with the layout. Sketch designs on scrap paper. After you have finished your sketch, start working on fabrics. What fabrics work for this? Do you have any favorite pieces of cloth that represent the family? A worn but loved tablecloth? An old baby blanket? Papa's shirt? A pair of baby pants or some other cloth of sentimental value? Look around to see what you can find. Perhaps let everyone select a piece that he or she feels represents him or her and work your design in sort of a quilt format.

Part Two

Now that you have drawn your design, you get to begin cutting the pieces. We've provided the directions for re-creating our design. Obviously, if you have your own design, these directions won't apply but the idea should be the same.

Steps

1. Cut the base and backing fabrics to 28" × 30".

2. The next step is to cut the background fabric into your desired shape. For best results, make yourself a paper pattern that is about 19" high by 18" wide. It is very easy to get a perfectly symmetrical pattern. Remember how you used to make paper hearts out of construction paper in elementary school? This is the same principle. Fold the paper in half lengthwise, then draw half of your shape. Cut along the lines and open up. If you don't like the shape, scrap it and try again until you are happy. Position the paper on the base just to see how the size and shape work for you. After you get the pattern just so, use it to cut your background fabric.

3. Trace the smaller name banner pattern from page 150 (or use your own label design) onto the paper side of the iron-on adhesive. Trace as many as you need for your family. Fuse to the wrong side of the appropriate fabric according to the manufacturer's recommendations. Cut out the labels around the outer lines. If you would like the scroll lines to show, hold the pieces up to a window and draw them on the right side of the fabric with a fabric marker (or mark them with a pencil for embroidery later on).

4. Repeat the process for the one large name label (use the pattern on page 150 or your own design).

5. Fold all of the edges of the background shape under ¼" to the wrong side and press.

6. Position the background piece in the center of the base piece, pin, and sew around all four edges. (You can go over this with a decorative stitch if you like. See how Kathie did it with the double running stitch?)

7. Cut your branches from the appropriate fabric. Use your own design, or follow these guidelines to achieve the tree shape as shown in the photo:

    a. Cut two 3½" × 19" strips.

    b. Place one strip in the middle of your background. Trim the strip to fit the shape at the top and bottom.

    c. Cut the other strip freehand, as shown, to create the side branches with smaller branches at the ends. Remember, branches are organic and don't have to be a specific size or shape.

8. Position your tree trunk and branches onto the background (branches under the trunk if you are using our design), pin it in place, and stitch around the edges.

9. You can see Kathie has done freeform machine stitching to create bark for her trunk. It's a nice touch, but it's totally optional.

This is a good stopping point. So, take a break. Have a glass of water, chocolate milk, or beer. Whatever fits your mood (and the time of day, of course).

Part Three

You can see your talisman coming to life. Have your children start thinking about things that represent the people they are right now. The clear pockets are meant to hold things that are important to each person or that the person feels is representative of him or her. The idea is that each pocket holds one item at a time, but the item can be swapped out at will. Examples of items that might work include a ribbon from a club or team,

a hand-drawn picture, a photograph, or a report card or certificate. It should be something positive, something you each want to share and something that makes the person feel good when he or she sees it in the pocket. That's part of the magic.

Steps

1. On the small name banners, create each person's name using letter stamps or fabric markers. If you like, you can also hand embroider the names or use your sewing machine to create the letters after the labels are fused into place.

2. On the large name banner, create your family's last name, once again either using stamps, fabric markers, or, like Kathie's banner, do hand-embroidered lettering (but wait until after the next step if you're embroidering).

Note: *See the tip on page 139 for information on using fabric stamps.*

3. Position the banners as you like. Fuse them in place and stitch around the edges. Embroider on the scroll lines and the lettering, if desired.

4. Cut one 5½" × 6" piece of the clear vinyl for each member of the family. (Or, if you've decided to make one collective pocket, you can do that, too.)

5. Position one clear pocket on your banner. Place a piece of tracing paper on top of the plastic (the tracing paper is used to give your machine an easier time of gliding over the sticky vinyl. If you have a trusty method of sewing with vinyl please feel free to opt out of using the tracing paper and use whatever method suits your fancy). Place pins in the tracing paper around the edges of the plastic so that the paper is pinned to the fabric under pockets. (Doing it this way keeps you from puncturing the plastic). Stitch around the edge of the pocket using a zigzag stitch.

6. Pull the tracing paper off.

7. Repeat Steps 5 and 6 with the other pockets.

8. Add any other appliqués, embroidery designs, or decorative elements as you see fit.

9. Put your completed piece on your work surface and have a look. What shape appeals to you? Do you want to leave it rectangular? Want to cut away the bottom corners? Really look at it. Talk about the design with your kids. If you do trim it, cut the backing piece to the same shape by laying the pieces together with the wrong sides facing.

10. Cut four 5½" × 6" strips of the backing/tab fabric. These are the loops for hanging the talisman.

11. Fold the strips in half lengthwise with the right sides together and stitch ¼" from the aligned raw edges.

12. Turn the strips right side out and press them flat.

13. Topstitch the strips ⅛" from the long edges.

14. Fold the strips in half lengthwise (short raw edges touching) to make your loops. Position and pin them along the top of your banner as illustrated.

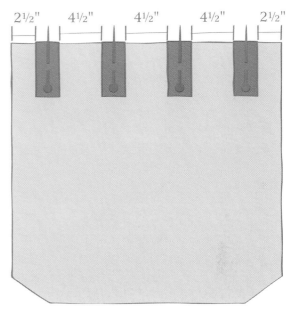

15. Place your back piece on top of the banner with the right sides facing and stitch along the top edge only, using a ½" seam allowance.

16. Flip the back piece over the top so it is now on the back of the banner and press along the top.

17. If needed, trim the edges of the banner and the back piece to make them even.

18. Apply the bias tape as described on page 139.

Ta-da! You did it. Now find a prominent place in your front entry or on your front door to hang your creation. Remember to swap out the pocket contents on a random or regular basis as a way of keeping the talisman and all it represents in your consciousness. You might try a weekly or monthly changing of contents with one person assigned the duty of gathering items from each family member. Do whatever works for your family.

Each time you enter your home, take a minute, take a breath, and remember that you are home. And that's a good thing.

Family Records Book

Before we go on about this project, we'd like to tell a little story . . .

We had a vision for this project long before we actually made it. We thought of it as part family scrapbook and part family registry kind of thing—you know, like in the olden days when families recorded all the family history and information in a Bible? Although this book was to be a lot less formal, the idea of having all our information in one giant, accessible place remained the same. Throughout our collective years of parenting, we have come up with some good family blessings and customs. We practice random acts of ritual and tradition and our families say some funny and poignant things that we'd kind of like to record for all time—or at least for the time being. We liked the old style scrapbooks that people kept—the kind our moms had in college made of heavy brown paper, where things were printed and pasted in, old love letters on store-bought stationary were stored in little glued pockets, and funny pictures of friends were affixed with modest witticisms and the like.

So, for our book that was to be a modern representative of things past, we thought it'd be great to use a big old book such as an outdated atlas or encyclopedia or some other large, hard-backed tome that was no longer really valid as a book but still attractive as an object. Our public library system has a Recycled Reads bookstore, so we traveled north of the river in search of the perfect book that would serve as the base for our project.

As we arrived we realized the bookstore was closed for the day. Bummer. As we are familiar with the many thrift stores in our town, we racked our brains for ideas for a store that was nearby. There was a large Goodwill store down the street that offered a good selection of random, reasonably priced stuff. So we went. As we walked in we were struck by how big and organized their book section was. Bingo! We knew we'd find what we were looking for here. As we looked for what we thought we were seeking, we realized, hmm, maybe not. The pages were too this and the binding was too that and we just weren't feeling it. So we scoured the shelves for inspiration, and we found it.

Boxed record collections. Tons of them, from all genres and eras. They had a pull-out form similar to file folders, and they were in a flat box that opened like a gift to reveal all the beautiful folders of records inside. They were hard-backed books with lovely sturdy, heavy-duty paper that was completely reminiscent of the scrapbook in our memories. We knew we'd found our base for our project.

That afternoon our friend Liz came over. She's won a Caldecott so she has a way with words that is like pure poetry. She took one look at the record box and said, "Oh, cool. Family Records." And there you have it. The story of our Family Records project and how it came from its original idea to be what you see here in these pages. Further proving the idea that all is as it should be.

Perhaps you're looking at it and thinking, "Well, where am I going to get one of those?" If you have a thrift store or a used record store near you, that's where you should first look. Boxed record sets had a huge heyday back in the day (that same day as those cool scrapbooks everyone kept). There were boxed record sets of all varieties for every kind of music lover from the 78s to the 33s and maybe even the 45s. There are so many that as you look for yours, you might even be able to get picky with what kind of music matches your family's style. If you look and look and still don't find a boxed record set, look online. Or, maybe, just maybe, you can email us and we'll find one for you. Or you can make it yourself using an old book or some file folders, or one of those old scrapbooks from long ago.

The purpose of the Family Records book is to give you a mechanism for honoring your family and marking your family's place in this world. It can hold all your witticisms, blessings, traditions, and memories in one beautiful place. It has pockets for storing scraps of inspiration and journal pages for logging lessons learned and family-isms. It has a pocket and prompts for helping you figure out your family's mission. It has other special pockets for keeping mementos of birthdays, holidays, and all your special occasions. It even has room for writing stuff about your regular days.

You might be thinking, "It's too late for us to start this kind of thing. Our kids are too big, and we've already missed too much." Nonsense. Right now is always a great time to start. Right now. And if you missed that moment, then how about right now? Or right now? (We've been hanging out with fourth graders too much.) Our point is, just start now and you won't miss anything else.

We've provided detailed instructions for making your own Family Records Book, but this project is very much open to your own creative interpretations. Play around. Incorporate your family's collective ideas, talents, and aesthetics. Make it yours.

Note: *We mention tailoring fabric choices and the like to your family's needs in a lot of our projects, but for this one especially we really want to emphasize that you should lay things out in a way that matches your style and your needs. We want you to use our ideas and at the same time create something that is completely your own. It's your family.*

• **Finished Measurements:** 13" × 13" •

Supplies

1 boxed record holder, large book, scrapbook, or binder

Note: *If you don't use a boxed record holder, you will also need some folders to use as pockets in your book. Try using red fiber expanding file pockets or even manila pocket binder dividers. You just have to adjust the layout accordingly, paying attention to where the pocket opens. For example, on the expanding pockets, the opening is on the side, so you should lay out your design accordingly, making the side of the binder the top of the project. The pocket dividers don't have a full-page pocket but still offer the possibility of storage for various items. If you want to get clever, you could also try playing around with album covers. Find covers that resonate with your family's themes. Hole punch the covers so that they can be placed in a three-ring binder. Even though the album covers are bigger than the binder, it could still serve as an aesthetically pleasing book with the oversized album "pages" sticking out the sides of the binder.*

Decoupage medium

Hard-coat decoupage medium, polyurethane, or clear acrylic spray

One old map or another aesthetically pleasing paper that you can cut up

Cutting mat

2 or 3 pieces of 60- or 80-pound paper in different colors (in our sample, Paper A is black and Paper B is gray)

2 or 3 25" pieces of various fabric trim such as rickrack, edge tape, and so on

Hobby knife

Tracing paper

2 paint brushes or foam brushes, one small for detail work and one a bit bigger

Part One

Determining what to put in your book is very much an unfolding of ideas. The pockets in our Family Records Book are

★ Family-isms: A collection of sayings, family mantras, cheers, or quotable quotes.

★ Blessings: A collection of blessings we say, including all the ways we feel completely blessed.

★ Rituals: What we do on birthdays, holidays, and special occasions as well as rituals we have in daily life. These might change from year to year or event to event; if they do, chronicle

them here. For example, on Christmas Day Bernadette's family takes a bike ride around town and has a picnic in the park. A short write-up of the day's events creates a nice family history.

★ Family mission: On our Future Craft Collective website, there is a link to Slow Family Living's family mission workbook. Download it. Fill it out. Keep it in here as a reminder of what makes your family, your family.

★ Annual review: A state-of-the-union kind of thing. What are you all doing? What do you like? Where have you been? You can create an annual family snapshot with words or images.

These are the sections that hold what we need. Do our ideas work for you? If so, copy them. If not, figure out what you need for your family's book. Maybe a list of places you've traveled? Perhaps a guest book of the people who have stayed in your home?

A family round-table discussion is a good way to come up with your family's pockets. Here are a few questions and writing prompts to get you started:

1. What do you like?

2. What holidays do you celebrate?

3. What are some of your birthday traditions?

4. Do you have dinner blessings or blessings at other times of day? If you don't now, do you want to?

5. Do you have any rituals around daily life? Morning? Weekends? Dinner rituals? Want to make some up?

6. This next exercise is taken from the Slow Family Living workbook. It's a way of figuring out not only what works but how you can create more of those moments that work well. Think of a moment in family life when you thought, "Ah, this is what family life is all about!" Can you break it down into elements? This is less about the "where" and the "when" and more about the "what." What are you doing? How are you feeling? What elements are involved? Make a list. Can you bring some of these elements into daily life?

7. Do you have any family sayings or expressions? Do your kids ever say things that you wish you could remember for posterity?

8. Go around the circle and have everyone write down a word that they feel describes family life.

9. Come up with a collective word that the whole family agrees on.

10. What parts of the day do you feel might need a little extra ritual around them?

11. What are ten things your family likes to do together?

Part Two

It's funny to give instructions for this project because we really want you to take it into your own hands. We've tried to be clear, while simultaneously being a tad bit vague.

After you've decided what materials you'll use, you can begin the layout. We've started with the cover to give you a visually pleasing piece right from the get-go.

We used paper cutting as our method for creating our words. You can also use stencils, rub-on letters, stickers, markers, or computer print-outs, anything you want. You can also have each member of the family participate in making a collage with cut-out or drawn letters and images. What best represents your family? Clean and modern? Old fashioned? Chaotic? Make it yours.

Steps

1. (For paper cutting) Write your words on tracing paper in thick letters. You might also want to add a "started" date, such as the year you became a family or got married. You'll be doing your cover words and also the wording for your inside pages.

2. Measure your map cover piece (or whatever decorative paper you've chosen) according to the book you're using. For example, our cover is 13" × 14" so we cut a map piece that is 26½" × 11", big enough to wrap all the way around top to bottom and to the inside, leaving a 1½" border on each side. We wrapped it and then marked with a pencil where our cover wording and design should go.

3. Spread your map out on the cutting mat (or thick piece of cardboard) and place the tracing paper where you have marked the words to be placed. Lightly brush the decoupage medium on the corners to hold the tracing paper in place. Do the same for the inside words using another piece of map paper.

4. Use the craft knife to cut out your words from both the tracing paper and the map. It's tricky but satisfying. Save the letters you cut out! You can use these on the book's spine.

5. If you feel your cut out letters don't stand out enough against the color of your book cover, you might want to accentuate your letters by placing a piece of contrasting paper behind your map paper. We used black backing paper on our book. Just dab a bit of the decoupage medium around the back of the cut out letters and place your map paper on top of your contrasting color paper. This step will vary according to your aesthetic desires and the materials you are using.

6. Wrap the box cover in the map paper as shown in the sample. (The map wraps around both the inside and the outside of the cover, so make sure to cut a piece large enough to cover both.) Brush the decoupage medium on the back of the map, and attach the map to the cover. Wrap the edges of the map around to the inside of the box and join the two ends.

Note: *Give the decoupage medium some time to dry between steps.*

7. Arrange your other embellishments, such as rickrack, edge trim, or any other fabric trim, on the cover and use the decoupage medium to hold them in place. This is a good way to hide paper edges that look unfinished or to shore up weaknesses in the construction of the base material (the record box). We used a twill tape trim on the folded edges of the record box's spine because there were some splits beginning to appear.

8. Brush decoupage medium over the whole cover to give it a decoupage look.

9. Coat all decoupaged areas with a layer of hard-coat decoupage medium or polyurethane or acrylic spray to diminish stickiness.

10. Cut another piece of map to be used as a pocket on the inside of the front cover. We cut ours to $10\frac{1}{2}$" × 15" and folded the paper in half the long way so that the pocket is a double thickness and sized $10\frac{1}{2}$" × $7\frac{1}{2}$".

11. Stitch the paper for the pocket all the way around the outside edges using a basting stitch.

12. Brush decoupage medium on both sides of the paper. After the glue has dried, coat it with a hard-coat decoupage medium, polyurethane, or acrylic spray. Let it dry.

13. Brush the decoupage medium on the side and bottom edges of your pocket and glue it inside the book cover.

That's it for your cover. And for Part Two. Now go water the garden. Breathe in some fresh air for your brain, which is surely tweaked after that process.

Part Three

In this part we work on the embellishment of the interior pockets. You can see we totally capitalized on the "record" idea with this one. In addition to adding some design elements, this next part is also

about covering up the holes that allow the records to be seen. You need to do more paper cutting either with a blade or scissors. This can look however you like, and you can go with our theme of records or not. And if you use something other than the boxed record set, you won't have a hole to cover. You could even just cut the words and forget the circles altogether.

Steps

Note: *If you're using a three-ring binder instead of the boxed record set we used, it may already have an inside pocket that you can embellish, or you can decorate expanding file pockets or manila pocket dividers. If you're using a different alternative, you can glue pockets inside the cover or perhaps skip these pockets altogether.*

1. For each pocket cut two 4" diameter circles from Paper A.

2. For each pocket cut two 32" diameter circles from Paper B.

3. For each pocket cut two 2½" diameter rings from Paper A.

4. If you haven't already cut all your words from Paper A in Step 4 of Part Two, cut out the rest of your words now. Again use the tracing paper and blade method or utilize another method. Even simple ransom note lettering collaged from magazines can look pretty cool. You can also use the letters you saved (remember those?) to put on the book's spine or elsewhere.

5. Stack your circles in this order: the Paper A 4" circle on bottom, the Paper B 3" circle in the middle, and the Paper A ring on top, putting just a dab of glue on each to hold them in place.

6. Brush the decoupage medium over the top of the stack.

Note: *Remember to let your decoupage medium dry between steps!*

7. Cover the stack with a layer of hard-coat decoupage medium, polyurethane, or acrylic spray.

8. Put a thin line of decoupage medium on the outside perimeter of your stack of circles.

9. Open the folder and carefully use the decoupage medium to glue the circle into place. Make sure you don't accidently glue the folder shut!

10. When the decoupage medium has dried, repeat Steps 5 through 9 for the back circle.

11. Use words and any other design elements to embellish the inside of the book.

Simple, right? That's it for the pockets. And really that's it for the crafting part.

After your book is complete you can start figuring out what goes in the pockets. Will you use notebooks? A sweet handmade journal? A composition book? Sheets of paper from random life events? This method is kind of fun in that pulling pages out one-by-one gives the book sort of a treasure chest feel. If you like a little more organization, you might want a proper notebook to keep things in chronological order.

Keep your book in a visible spot. Take it out on occasion to add to or embellish. Give it a place of honor and develop a ritual for reviewing it. It will become a beautiful chronicle of your family's place in this world and your commitment to each other. It'll also be a fun way to while away a family afternoon. Just think, when all your kids are grown and moved out, you can peruse the memories held in your Family Records Book and savor the sweetness of it all. And most likely, your kids will use some of the very same rituals and customs with their own families. That's how traditions are born!

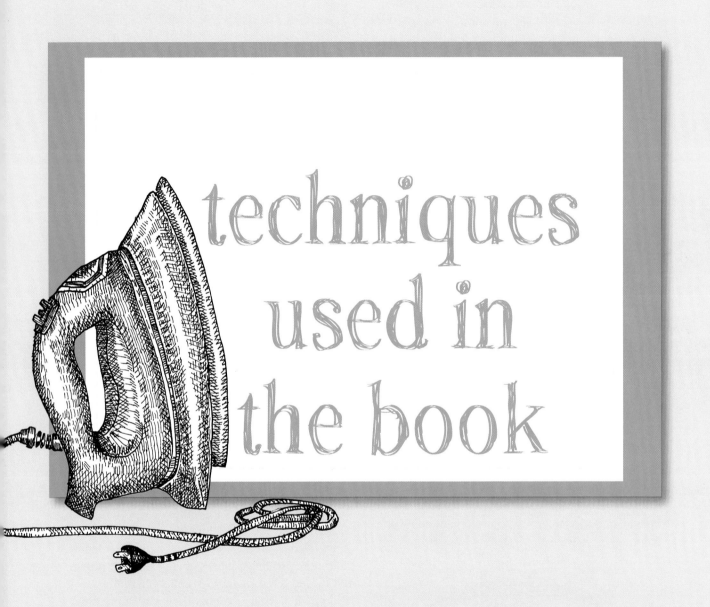

techniques used in the book

Some techniques are used in more than one project in this book,
so we've gathered them here for easy reference.

Working with Bias Tape

1. Starting in the middle of one edge on the back of the project, position the raw edge of the bias tape, laying it so that the tape falls away from the circle.

2. Approximately 4" from the end of the bias tape, start stitching the tape to the project. As you stitch around the project, move the tape into position. Stop stitching approximately 4" from the other end.

3. Fold the unsewn edge over the edge of the project.

4. Flip your project over and fold the raw edge under so that it can be sewn underneath the edge of the tape to camouflage it.

5. Stitch the second edge as described in Step 3 (again leaving loose approximately 4" on each end). Be sure to keep the folded edge tucked under as you sew.

6. Lay one of the loose 4" ends in place along the edge of the project and then lay the second loose end in place. Where the second end meets the first, make a crease.

7. Measure 2" from the crease on the second loose end and cut.

8. Unfold both loose ends and place them together at a right angle with the good sides facing. Pin them in place and then stitch with a diagonal seam. (See the illustration.)

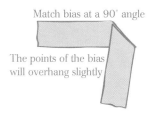

Match bias at a 90° angle

The points of the bias will overhang slightly

Stitch a diagonal seam and trim to ¼"

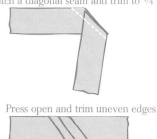

Press open and trim uneven edges

9. Trim the seam allowance to ¼" and press it open with your fingers.

10. Fold the bias tape along its original fold and align it along the edge of the project so that you can finish stitching on one side. Fold the other half of the tape to the other side of the project and hand-stitch it in place.

Note: *If you want an excellent tutorial on finishing binding ends, visit http://www.allpeoplequilt.com/techniques/finishing/index.html. You can find this information and all sorts of other helpful tips and tricks on the All People Quilt site.*

Tying Buttons

1. Center your button at the desired position.

2. Insert the embroidery floss into the needle.

3. Insert the needle into the button and the fabric through the top side.

4. Pull the floss through a few inches, but leave a long tail.

5. Insert the needle into the fabric then through the button on the bottom side.

6. Pull through until the tail is about 2" long.

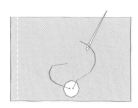

7. Trim the other end of the floss down to about 2".

8. Tie the ends together in a double knot.

9. Trim the ends to the desired length.

Fabric Stamping

1. Mix the fabric paint with just a tiny bit of water in a shallow dish. A large yogurt top works well as a dish for the paint.

2. Place the fabric right side up on your work surface.

3. Brush each stamp with a bit of the fabric paint.

4. If you haven't stamped before, practice first on a scrap piece of fabric before you stamp your words on your project.

pattern pieces

Blessing and Sharing Pouch Pocket

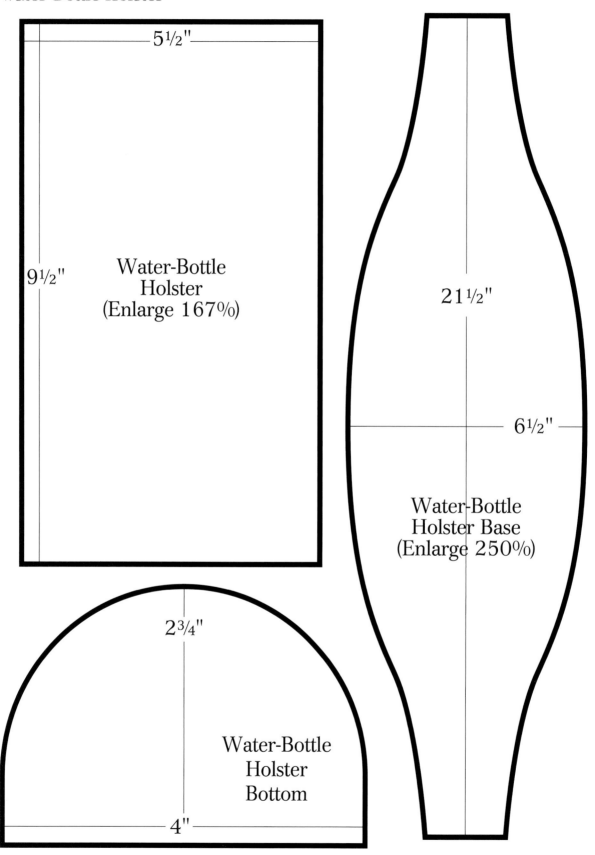

Water-Bottle Holster

5½"

9½"

Water-Bottle
Holster
(Enlarge 167%)

2¾"

Water-Bottle
Holster
Bottom

4"

21½"

6½"

Water-Bottle
Holster Base
(Enlarge 250%)

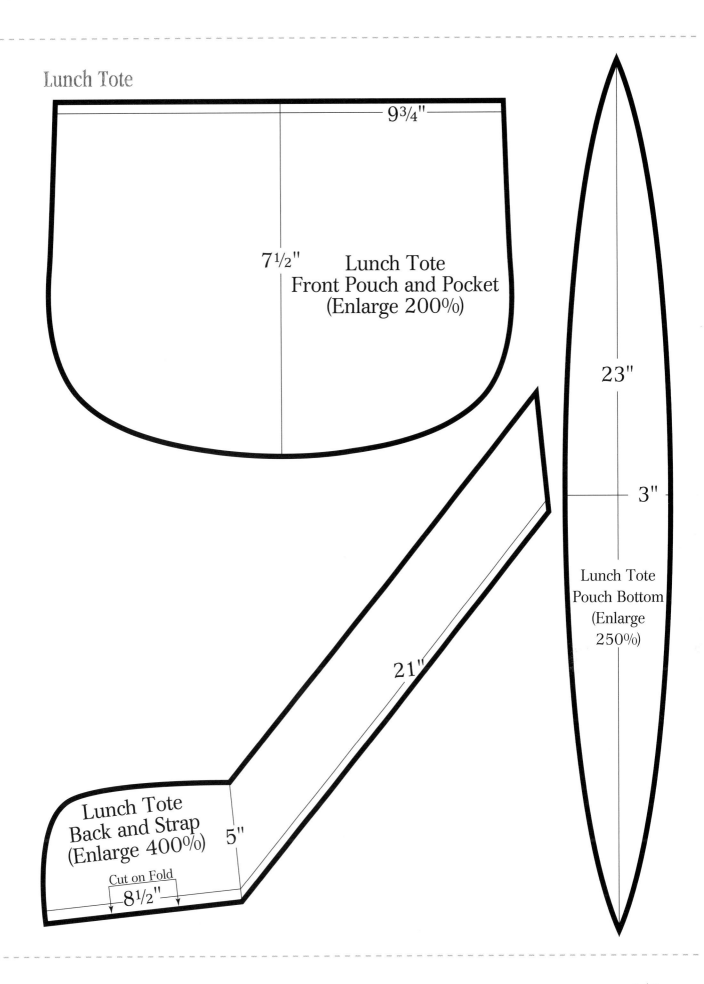

Lunch Tote

9¾"

7½"   Lunch Tote
Front Pouch and Pocket
(Enlarge 200%)

23"

3"

Lunch Tote
Pouch Bottom
(Enlarge
250%)

21"

Lunch Tote
Back and Strap
(Enlarge 400%)   5"

Cut on Fold
8½"

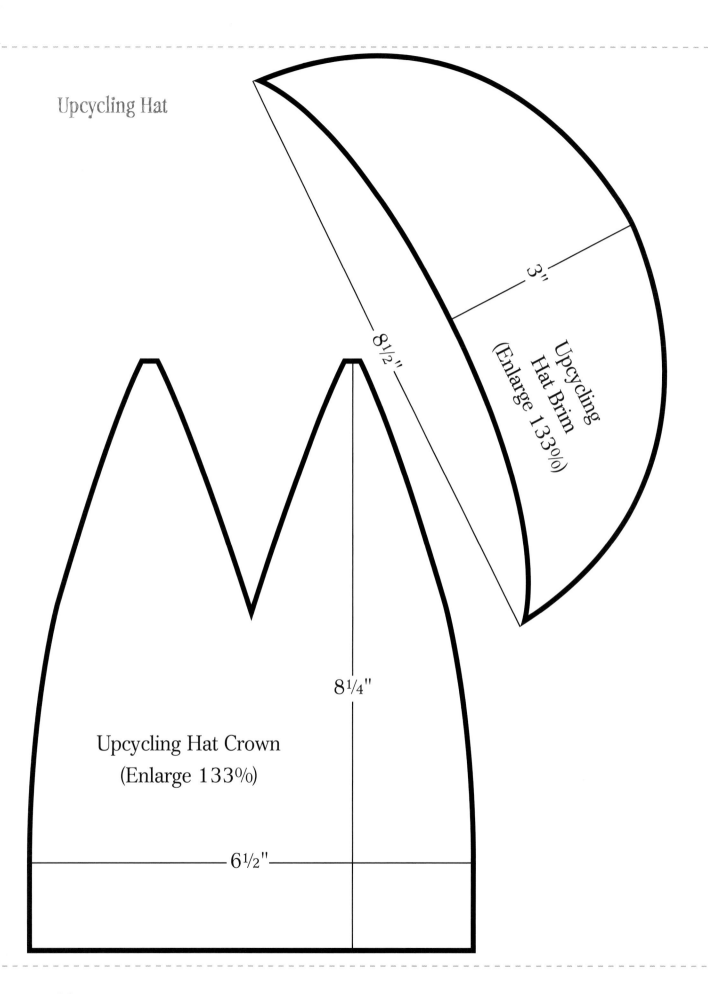

Upcycling Hat

3"

Upcycling
Hat Brim
(Enlarge 133%)

8½"

8¼"

Upcycling Hat Crown
(Enlarge 133%)

6½"

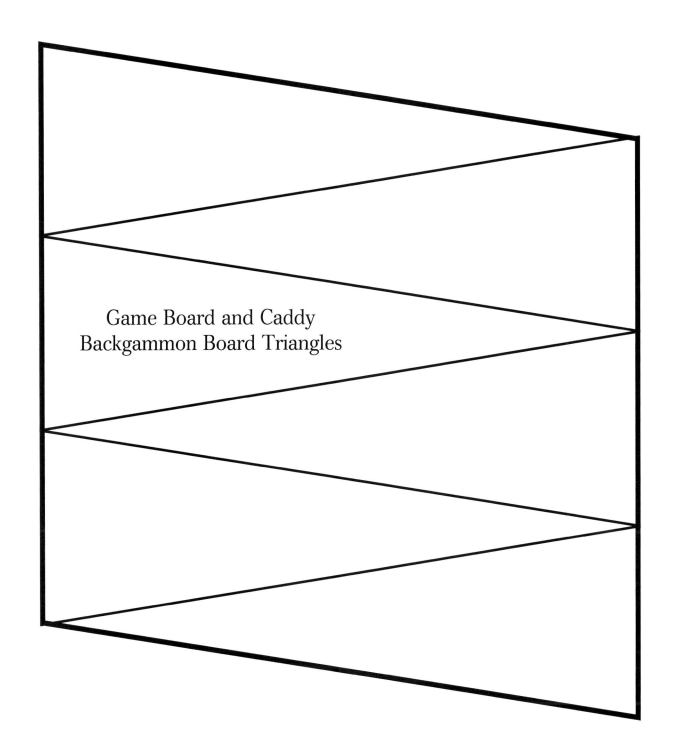

Game Board and Caddy
Backgammon Board Triangles

Juggling Balls in a Drawstring Sack

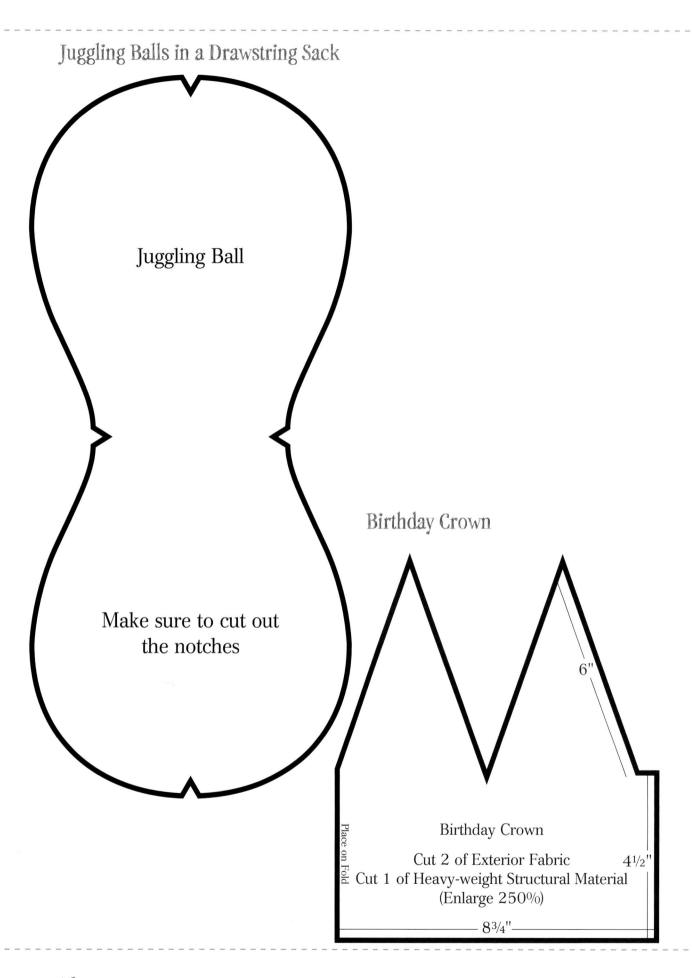

Juggling Ball

Make sure to cut out
the notches

Birthday Crown

Place on Fold

Birthday Crown

Cut 2 of Exterior Fabric

Cut 1 of Heavy-weight Structural Material
(Enlarge 250%)

6"

4½"

8¾"

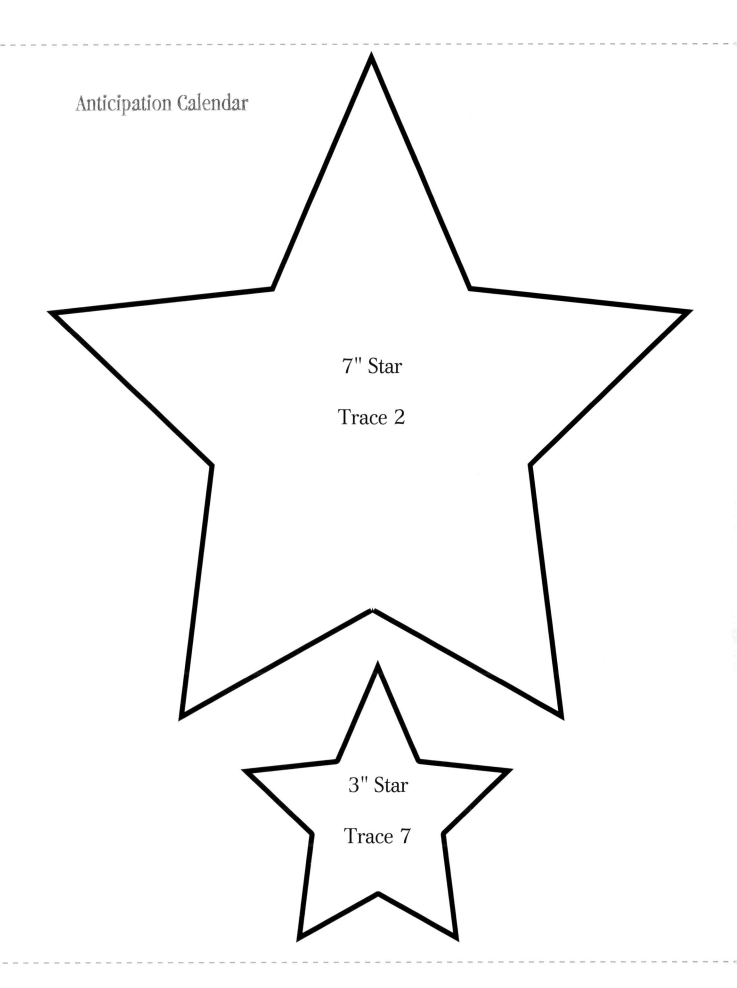

Anticipation Calendar

7" Star

Trace 2

3" Star

Trace 7

Pin the Tail on the Donkey

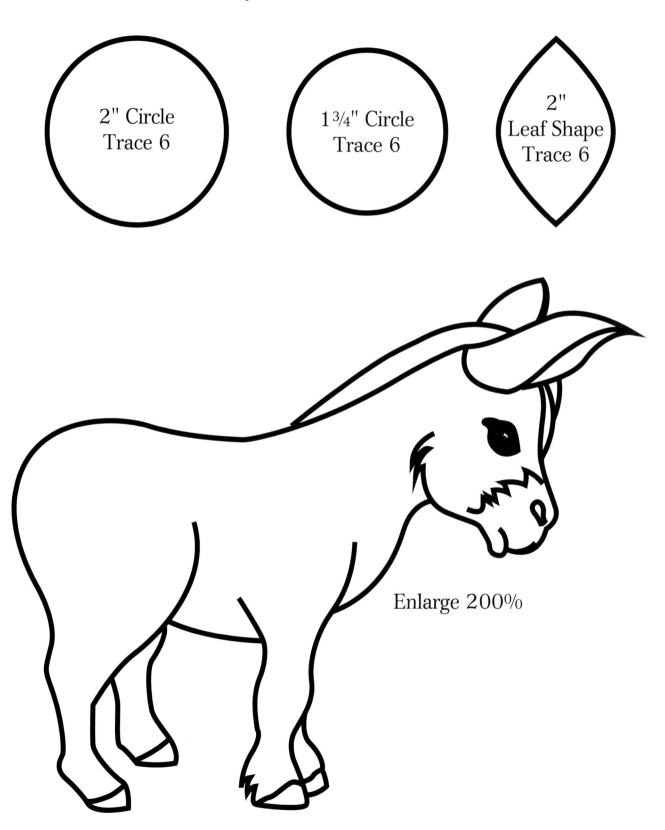

2" Circle
Trace 6

1 ¾" Circle
Trace 6

2"
Leaf Shape
Trace 6

Enlarge 200%

Family Flags

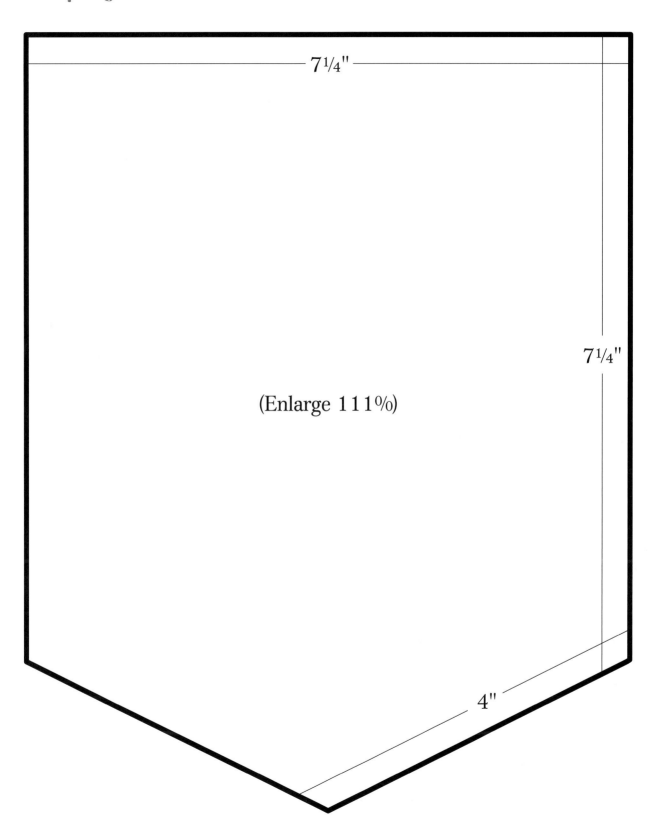

7¼"

7¼"

(Enlarge 111%)

4"

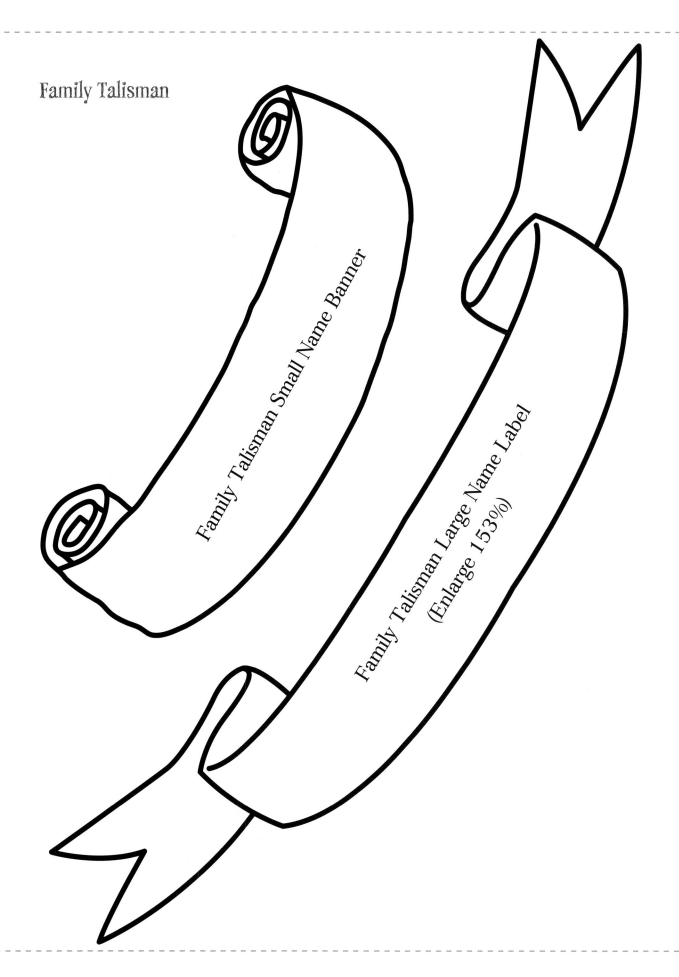

Family Talisman Small Name Banner

Family Talisman Large Name Label
(Enlarge 153%)

Index